About Island Press

Island Press is the only nonprofit organization in the United States whose principal purpose is the publication of books on environmental issues and natural resource management. We provide solutions-oriented information to professionals, public officials, business and community leaders, and concerned citizens who are shaping responses to environmental problems.

In 1994, Island Press celebrated its tenth anniversary as the leading provider of timely and practical books that take a multidisciplinary approach to critical environmental concerns. Our growing list of titles reflects our commitment to bringing the best of an expanding body of literature to the environmental community throughout North America and the world.

Support for Island Press is provided by The Geraldine R. Dodge Foundation, The Energy Foundation, The Ford Foundation, The George Gund Foundation, William and Flora Hewlett Foundation, The James Irvine Foundation, The John D. and Catherine T. MacArthur Foundation, The Andrew W. Mellon Foundation, The Pew Charitable Trusts, The Rockefeller Brothers Fund, The Tides Foundation, Turner Foundation, Inc., The Rockefeller Philanthropic Collaborative, Inc., and individual donors.

About the Trust for Public Land

The Trust for Public Land is a private, nonprofit land conservation organization that works nationwide to conserve land for people. Founded in 1972, the Trust for Public Land specializes in conservation real estate, applying its expertise in negotiation, public finance, and law to protect land for public use. Working with private landowners, communities, and government agencies, the Trust for Public Land has helped protect more than 1,000 special places nationwide for people to enjoy as parks, playgrounds, community gardens, recreation areas, historic landmarks, and wilderness lands. The Trust for Public Land also develops methods of land conservation and environmentally sound land use and shares this knowledge with urban and rural groups, local land trusts, and public agencies.

This handbook was prepared by the Conservation Services Program of the Trust for Public Land's Southeast Regional Office. Through this program, the Trust for Public Land provides technical assistance to help communities identify opportunities for parks and land protection.

About the National Trust for Historic Preservation

Since 1949, when the U.S. Congress chartered the National Trust for Historic Preservation as the only national, private, nonprofit organization with the responsibility of encouraging public participation in the preservation of sites, buildings, and objects significant in American history and culture, its constituency and programs have grown to match the need. Today, the National Trust serves 250,000 members, has seven regional offices, owns 18 historic house museums, and works with thousands of local community groups in all 50 states.

The National Trust's mission is to foster an appreciation of the diverse character and meaning of our American cultural heritage and to preserve and revitalize the livability of our communities by leading the nation in saving America's historic environments. Correspondingly, the National Trust's services have expanded to include heritage education, neighborhood revitalization, organizational development, legal advocacy, leadership training, and land conservation.

Since 1979, the Trust for Public Land and the National Trust have worked together to preserve historic buildings, archaeological sites, and scenic landscapes. In 1991, the National Trust awarded a Critical Issues Fund grant to TPL's Southeast Regional Office for the development of the *Views from the Road* handbook. This book represents the culmination of joint efforts between TPL and the National Trust in helping communities identify local natural and historic resources that must be protected.

Views from the Road

Views from the Road

A Community Guide for Assessing Rural Historic Landscapes

David H. Copps

A Project of the Trust for Public Land and
the National Trust for Historic Preservation

ISLAND PRESS
Washington, D.C. • Covelo, California

Library of Congress Cataloging-in-Publication Data

Copps, David H.
Views from the road: a community guide for assessing rural historic landscapes / David H. Copps.
p. cm.
Includes bibliographical references (p.) and index.
ISBN 1-55963-412-X (pbk.: acid-free paper)
1. Historic sites—United States—Conservation and restoration. 2. Landscape assessment—United States. 3. Historic preservation—United States. I. Title.
E159.C78 1995
363.6'9—dc20 95-12478
CIP

Printed on recycled, acid-free paper

Manufactured in the United States of America

10 9 8 7 6 5 4 3 2 1

Contents

Acknowledgments

This handbook was prepared by the staff of the Trust for Public Land, Southeast Regional Office, with grants from the National Trust for Historic Preservation's Critical Issues Fund, The Red Hills Conservation Program of Tall Timbers Research, Inc., and the Kentucky Heritage Council.

The Trust for Public Land would like to extend its special thanks to the following individual and foundations for their support, without which the publication of this handbook would not have been possible:

Miss Kate Ireland, George M. & Pamela S. Humphrey Fund, and Firman Fund

Co-author, Chapter Three, Handbook and Red Hills Case Study

Joy Dorst

Co-author, Chapters Four and Five (Handbook), Chapters One and Four (Red Hills Case Study)

Kevin McGorty

Co-author, Chapter One (Bluegrass Case Study)

Chris Amos

Editors

Kevin Mooney
Will Abberger

Handbook Design and Layout

Kevin Mooney

The Trust for Public Land, Southeast Regional Office

W. Dale Allen
Will Abberger
Kevin Mooney
David Copps

National Advisory Panel

Chris Amos
Marvin Collins
Grant DeHart
Jean Hocker
Diane Kane
Linda Flint McClelland
John Morgan
Jim Riggle
Sally Schauman
Samuel Stokes
Allen Stovall
Anthony C. Wood
Marty Zeller

National Trust for Historic Preservation - National Headquarters

Bridget Hartman
Shelley Mastran

National Trust for Historic Preservation - Southern Office

Susan Kidd
Daniel Carey

Tall Timbers Research, Inc.

Lane Green

Red Hills Conservation Association

Julie Moore

Red Hills Scenic Advisory Panel

Sallie Sullivan
Evelyn Meierkord
John Bulloch
Ted Thomas
Nancy Tinker
Ronny Hall
Herbert DeMott
John W. Fuller
Leon Neel
Lee Mitchell
Kevin McGorty
Linda Kay Williams
Mark Strickland

Kentucky Heritage Council

David Morgan
Susan Yessin

Bluegrass Scenic Advisory Panel

Donna Allen
Chris Amos
Don Ball
Toss Chandler
Ed Councill
Ned Crankshaw
Kim Klein
Chuck Knowles
Bonne Betz Loeb
Kate McCullough
David Morgan
Beth Stewart
Harold Tate

Photo Credits

Chris Amos: Figures 2.4, 2.12, 2.14, 2.16, 2.20, and 2.22.
David Copps: Figures 1.1, 1.2, 1.4, 1.5, 1.7, 2.5, 2.8, 2.11, 2.13, 2.17, 2.21, and 2.23.
Joy Dorst: Figures 1.10, 1.11, 2.1, 2.6, 2.15, and 2.18.
Courtesy of Kevin McGorty and the Historic Preservation Board: Figure 2.7.
James Valentine: Cover photo.
Susan Yessin: Figures 1.3, 2.2, and 3.4.

Views from the Road

INTRODUCTION

"Roads not only carry us from place to place, but many ... link us to the past, tracing patterns of movement across the landscape that are centuries old. ...They inspire a sense of discovery, beauty and neighborliness, in a world where roads have come to mean nothing more than a maddening gridlock of crass commercialism." [1]

Much as the family bible and old photo albums record family histories, America's rural countryside provides a living record of our collective past. The result of the long interaction between humans and nature, rural landscapes have been shaped over time by historical land use and management practices. These landscapes of heritage were formed by the activities and habits of past generations, and to the careful observer they offer a glimpse of long-forgotten lifestyles and traditions. The components, or characteristics, of the landscape our ancestors left behind—land use patterns, vegetation, buildings and structures, boundary demarcations, and circulation networks—not only give us insight into their beliefs and values, but create visual patterns which document their presence as surely as the discovery of archaeological treasures.

Unfortunately, the historical integrity and visual character of many rural landscapes are threatened by change. Residential and commercial development, the paving and widening of roads, and the routing of utility transmission corridors all contribute to their degradation. These changes are not intentional attempts to degrade important community resources. Rather, they are threats that occur for the most part because rural historic landscapes are poorly understood or identified. Until communities become more aware of these subtle landmarks and appreciate the remarkable stories they tell, protection measures aimed at preventing unintentional degradation will not follow and key cultural landmarks will continue to be unknowingly lost forever.

Increasing public awareness of rural historic landscapes is not an easy task. Historic preservation, the description under which rural landscape protection rightly falls, is usually perceived as simply an effort to save "old buildings." Campaigns to protect historic landscapes must first strive to broaden this perception, perhaps by stressing that historic landscapes are "old buildings" themselves, though designed and built not by one architect but hundreds, each adding to the other's work generation upon generation. Communities wishing to protect the visual character—the historical record—of their region's landscape must begin with this new twist to historic preservation.

The National Park Service (NPS) defines a rural historic landscape as "... a geographical area that historically has been used by people, or shaped or modified by human activity, occupancy, or intervention, and that possesses a significant concentration, linkage, or continuity of areas of land use, vegetation, buildings and structures, roads and waterways, and natural features." [2]

A few old barns such as this are all that remain of a once-thriving shade tobacco industry in North Florida.

Both logically and practically, a good starting point—the "point of departure"—for understanding, appreciating, and eventually protecting rural historic landscapes is from the network of public roads. People largely experience private, working lands from public roads and highways. These public places provide us with visual access to the countryside, where surrounding views reveal themselves as sequences of images which color our perception of the environment. Roads also provide important clues about early settlement patterns and historical patterns of movement across the land. In short, many of the roads that wind through these regions are themselves critical components of the historic landscape.

The first steps toward protecting the larger historic landscape should begin with a systematic assessment of the visual characteristics of the public road network and the development of sensible protection strategies. This undertaking is not only economically feasible for most communities, it also provides a framework for broader community planning issues.

In January of 1992, the Trust for Public Land (TPL), a national, nonprofit conservation organization, was awarded a Critical Issues Fund grant from the National Trust for Historic Preservation (NTHP) to provide rural and semi-urban communities with a method for identifying rural historic landscape resources for protection. TPL undertook the project with the intent of producing a product that combines key elements of traditional academic or professional historic landscape assessments—commonly used terminology, visual resource inventory techniques and analysis, etc.—with a practical understanding and attention to community capabilities and resources. The resulting hybrid methodology is rather unique, for it emphasizes grassroots community participation, adds meaning and depth to scenic evaluations by tying scenic resources to historic resources, and is relatively inexpensive.

Views from the Road: A Community Guide for Assessing Rural Historic Landscapes is a practical handbook for local land trusts, planning agencies, and other community organizations to use in preparing inventories of rural historic resources based on scenic roads. *Views* is meant to help communities integrate the visual and aesthetic qualities of rural road corridors with the history of land use to provide a rational basis for public and private land conservation efforts. Though the methodology may appear fairly complex upon first reading, all steps are quite do-able, particularly if professionals with experience in some of the tasks are able to participate. Studies completed using the *Views* methodology will help to (1) enhance public awareness and appreciation for the special landscape resources of rural historic regions, and (2) provide the necessary baseline information to plan protection strategies.

An old bridge along an abandoned route which once wound through the Red Hills.

This handbook is based primarily on two case studies. The central case study includes TPL's ongoing work to identify the visual character of more than 300 miles of public roads that wind through the Red Hills region of North Florida and South Georgia. The second case study features two historic and scenic routes in the Bluegrass Region of Kentucky, between Lexington and Frankfort. These studies are referred to throughout the handbook to provide practical examples of how each step of the methodology has been implemented.

Like any step-by-step guide, *Views from the Road* is not a "set-in-stone" manual. While the method described has been tested and refined in the two case studies, creative study teams are certainly encouraged to keep an eye out for shortcuts and alternatives. Users may find that the

Views methodology works better for them in some steps than in others, where it may be necessary to modify and adapt the method to suit project area needs. Read through all the steps and get a feel for the process in advance to note particular parts of the handbook that may need custom tailoring.

Also, carefully consider project goals before beginning any substantial information collection. While resource protection is indeed the focus of *Views*, different goals—tourism, economic development, recreation—are also important considerations for many communities. Early goal identification is essential because it will influence the types and level of information collected, as well as other elements of the study.

There are six chapters in *Views from the Road:* Context, Cultural Features, The Visual Experience, Inventory, Evaluation, and Protection Strategies and Techniques. Although each chapter builds on the material presented in the preceding chapter, it is not necessary that the handbook be used sequentially. For example, readers may already possess adequate historic resource information along their community roads and may only need to determine scenic resources (i.e., which landscape types contribute most to their community's visual character). If so, they may wish to skip Chapters 1 and 2, aimed at identifying historic resources, and begin with Chapter 3, "The Visual Experience." The handbook is intended to be useful as both a "start to finish" guide as well as a "pick and choose" reference.

Views is meant to help those most affected by irreversible changes to rural historic landscapes—the people who live there. State and federal preservation programs can sometimes help, but for now the passion and dogged determination to save these special places rests with people who know the bends in the roads, hail familiar landmarks as old friends, and feel dismay at the bulldozing of a favorite field. Common among many of these local preservation success stories are three elements: community teamwork, community input, and community consensus. Not surprisingly, those same elements form the basis for *Views from the Road.*

"Views" is meant to help communities integrate the visual and aesthetic qualities of rural road corridors with the history of land use to provide a rational basis for public and private land conservation efforts.

Scenic canopy roads in North Florida are products of the antebellum transportation network. Visually appealing today, they once provided shade that cooled cotton-laden wagons on their way to market in Tallahassee. (Photo courtesy of James Valentine.)

The method described in this handbook stresses community involvement and participation.

1

Context

Context is the setting within which the landscape has developed over time. Long-term climatic conditions, the influence of vegetation and wildlife, and the influences of people on the land all contribute to regional context.

A good starting point for learning about a rural historic landscape and its roads is to establish the context of the region. Context is the setting within which the landscape has developed over time. Long-term climatic conditions, the influence of vegetation and wildlife, and the influences of people on the land all contribute to the context of a region. It is helpful to define context in terms of physiography, ecology, and cultural history. Understanding the regional context in terms of the land and its inhabitants can be an important first step in developing an effective landscape protection program.

Physiographic Context

Learning about the physiographic characteristics of an area helps in the understanding of historical developments. Physiography is defined by such factors as soils, topography, broad patterns of vegetation, drainage patterns, and water resources. The way early settlers adapted to regional physiography greatly influenced the locations and configurations of rural communities.

One of the best resources available for determining physiographic context is the Soil Conservation Service Soil Survey Series. Available for most counties in the nation, soil surveys contain a wealth of information on geology, physiography, drainage, and vegetation. They can be obtained through local libraries or local Soil Conservation Service offices.

The Relationship of Roads to Physiography

The character of a road depends on how it relates to the lay of the land. On a future trip, note the way roads relate to topography. Compare the smooth flow of a road that follows the contour with the dramatic up and down (roller coaster effect) of an alignment perpendicular to the contours. The land determines the character of the road, from the winding and twisting paths cut through mountainous areas to the long straight stretches characteristic of low, level country (Fig. 1.1).

For the most part, old roads seem to follow the landscape and recall times past

Figure 1.1
A road alignment as it relates to the lay of the land in the Red Hills.

Figure 1.2
Antebellum roads in the Red Hills were worn down to their present levels by mule-drawn wagons hauling cotton to market.

Negative Ecological Impacts of Roads

More important than the ecological value of roads is their impact upon the environment. Habitat disruption, water pollution from runoff, and the killing of wildlife by motorists are the most apparent impacts (Fig. 1.4). Less apparent are the indirect costs of air pollution associated with automobile emissions.

Questions to Ask

What are the various plant and animal communities within the study area?

How do the roads in the study area impact the ecological communities? Describe both negative and positive impacts.

Historical Context

Establishing historical context helps in the understanding of a rural historic landscape's overall significance and integrity by providing key background information about patterns of prior human settlement and land use. It offers insight into broad themes, or trends, and related periods of history. For example, the historic periods of the Red Hills region include the Prehistoric, Spanish Contact and Settlement, Colonial, Antebellum, Reconstruction, and the Early Twentieth Century; a major theme tying these periods together is the influence of agricultural activities on the landscape.

Historical Context of the Road Network

The very nature of roads as linkages between places where people wished to travel establishes their importance as historic landscape elements. Virginia Beach, of South Carolina's Low Country Open Land Trust, captures the essence of roads as a historical feature:

> *Roads not only carry us from place to place, but many … link us to the past, tracing patterns of movement across the landscape that are centuries old. Whether guided by the "lay of the land," human settlement patterns, the marketplace, or a combination of such influences, these old roads are a critical link to our sense of community and our sense of place. They inspire a sense of discovery, beauty and neighborliness, in a world where roads have come to mean nothing more than a maddening gridlock of crass commercialism (Fig. 1.5).*

"Roads are built to connect places that people want to travel between…It is a riddle that contains its own answer, because old roads are textbooks of history and geography. The road tells the attentive traveler about a part of the region's past that may not be reflected in historic buildings or landscape features."[4]

Figure 1.5 *A leisurely trip down an old road can inspire the sense of exploration and discovery in all of us.*

Questions to Ask

What is the sequence of historic periods and related themes which contribute to the significance of the region?

What is the historical significance of the network of public roads throughout the region?

What were the major influences on the development of the pattern that exists today?

Red Hills Case Study

The heart of the Red Hills quail plantation belt lies between Thomasville, Georgia, and Tallahassee, Florida. Although other game bird preserves extend as far north as Albany, Georgia, the greatest concentration of plantations, encompassing nearly 300,000 acres, stretch along a 38-mile belt containing the northern portions of Leon and Jefferson Counties in Florida, and the southern half of Thomas County and southeastern section of Grady County in Georgia (Fig. 1.6).

The region is known as the Red Hills because of its rolling hills and reddish sandy loam and rich clay soils. The red soils are most visible on the cut banks along the area's canopy roads. The hill country is in sharp contrast to the flatwoods that dominate the lower coastal plain south of Tallahassee.

Seasonal rainfall averages 60 inches, with a subtropical climate in summer and temperate climate in winter. The land is drained by a dendritic pattern of numerous small streams and groundwater seepage into limestone aquifers. The major lakes of the region include Jackson, Iamonia, Foshalee, Miccosukee, and Lafayette. In addition to these large shallow basins there are abundant cypress-gum swamps and small limesink lakes which dot the landscape.

Once part of the great 70 million acre longleaf pine forest that extended from Texas to Virginia, the Red Hills contains some of the South's few remaining parcels of old growth longleaf pine and wiregrass communities. Like most of the South, however, the virgin longleaf forest in the region succumbed to cultivation, timbering, and the suppression of fire which it

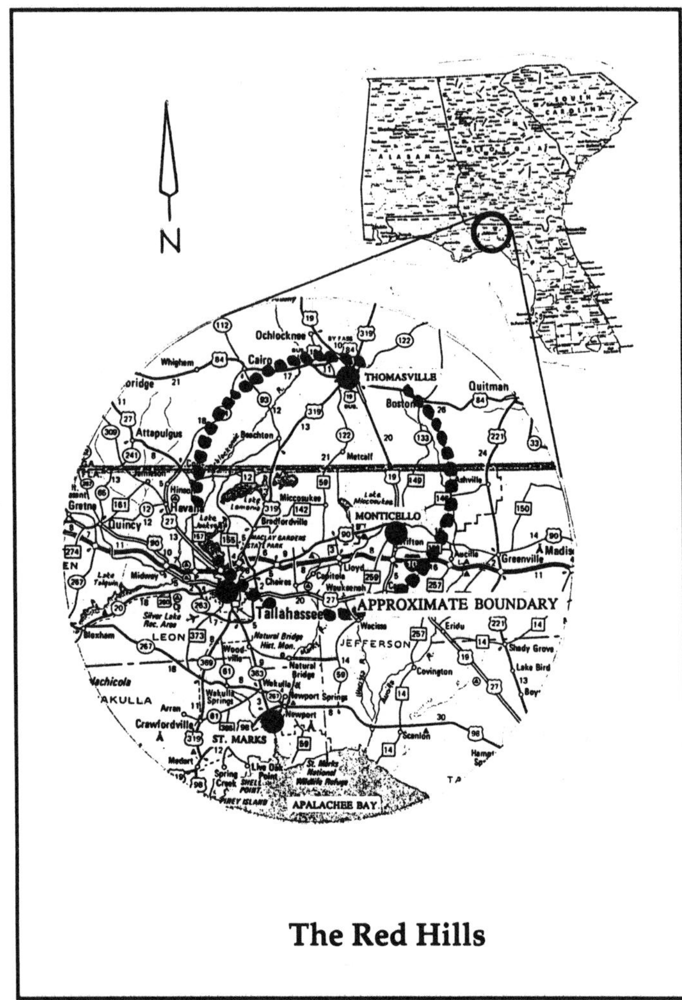

Figure 1.6 *Red Hills Locator Map.*

Figure 1.7 *Park-like stands of pine, a characteristic vegetative pattern in the Red Hills.*

requires for regeneration. Today, the traveler experiences a landscape of secondary successional growth of shortleaf and loblolly pines and oaks in the uplands (Fig. 1.7). Distinct hardwood forests exist in the magnolia-beech communities, commonly referred to by early writers as the "high hammocks" and pine-oak-hickory forests.

The Red Hills is rich in biological diversity. The endangered red-cockaded woodpecker and gopher tortoise join 85 other threatened species found in the Red Hills. Rich in plant and animal life, the region is a "bio-reserve" with habitat corridors for ranging mammals and migratory birds.

Majestic canopy roads wind past wildflower and fern covered pine parklands which are maintained through annual prescribed burning.

> *... [T]he bumpy North Florida roads [are] bordered by pines and sweetgums to which have been tacked stern warnings against poaching. In spring the wild plums bloom in white ribbons. Ditches are heavy in fall with bright beautyberries. Sometimes in the distance you catch a glimpse of a white mansion, or a vine-framed lake, or some upland hills whose sparse grasses are littered with pinestraw and cones. Maybe you will flush a quail covey of your own ahead of your car. The quail country has been tamed, but the ordered disorder of its wilderness is always full of life and sound.*[5]

When local writer Gloria Jahoda penned these words in 1966, many of the Red Hills country roads were unpaved, and many remain unpaved to this day. These old roads are not only the gateways to communities of the Red Hills, but the routes to its history (Fig. 1.8).

The public roadways pass small villages, churches, scattered abandoned tenant dwellings, and other historic resources that link the region to its past, but it is on the dirt back roads, however, that the traveler experiences a visual sense of history. Along these narrow winding roads it has taken centuries for travelers to cut ravines as much as twelve feet deep to form the red clay embankments. Lining the road are majestic live oaks. They

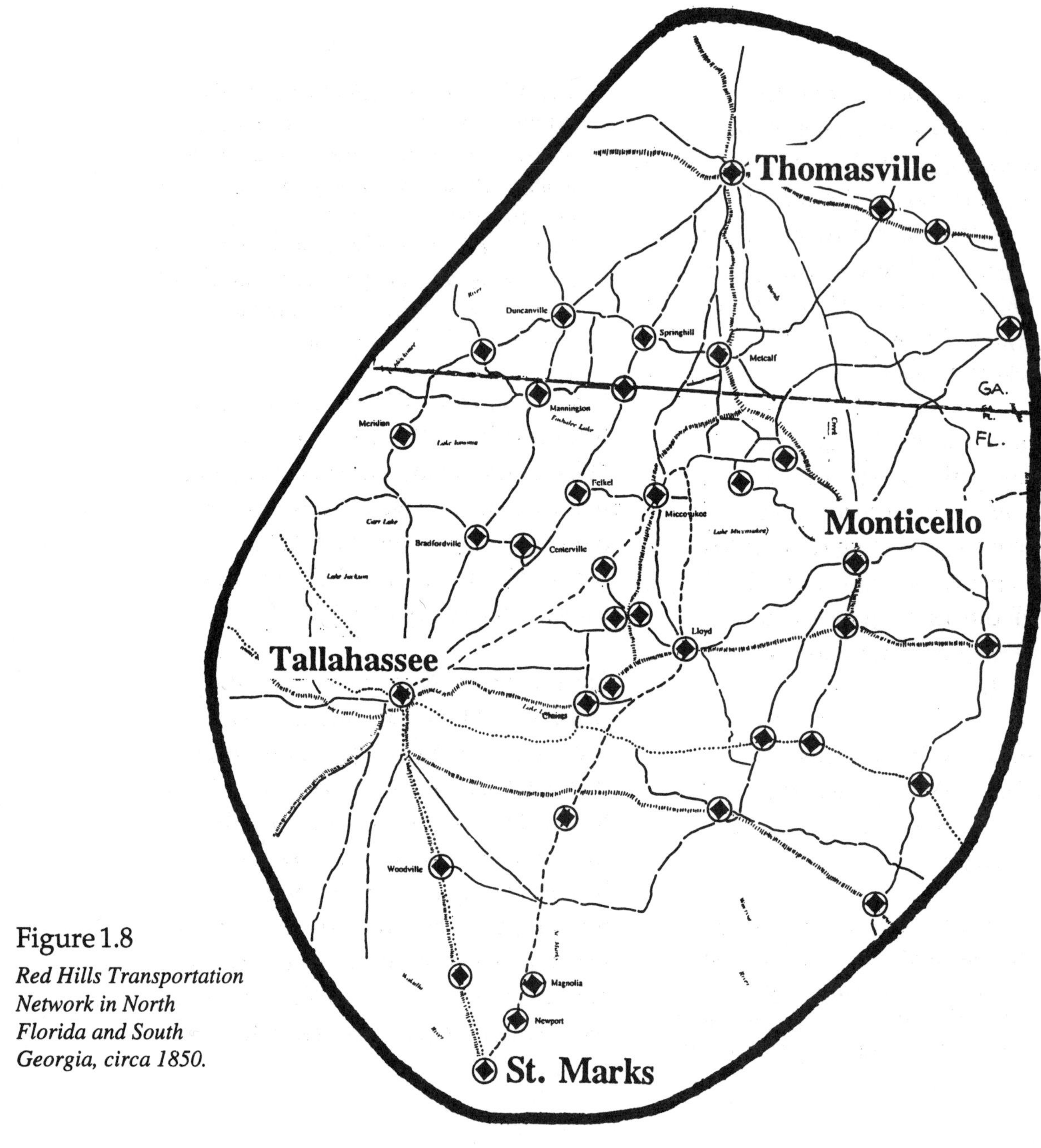

Figure 1.8

Red Hills Transportation Network in North Florida and South Georgia, circa 1850.

provide a cathedral-like tunnel of green that once shaded and cooled the cotton wagon hauler some 150 years ago.

The history of the Red Hills is the history of a unique landscape, shaped and designed by natural and human forces. For approximately 10,000 years, the Red Hills region has been inhabited. Each culture that has occupied the area has left an imprint on the land. Native Americans constructed large and highly sophisticated ceremonial mound centers, while Spanish explorers and friars established a trail of agricultural based missions. Antebellum cotton planters and their slaves, yeoman and tenant farmers, and more recently the northern game-bird hunters developed agricultural complexes, traces of which remain today.

The cultural landscape reveals archaeological sites of ancient civilizations. More recent history is identified through some of the South's finest architectural resources reflecting the prosperity, decline, and resurgence of the region's agricultural and hunting traditions. Many of these historic sites, buildings, and districts are listed in the National Register of Historic Places.

Bluegrass Case Study

The Bluegrass has been divided into three subregions by geographers: the Inner Bluegrass, the Eden Shale Belt, and the Outer Bluegrass (Fig. 1.9). The focus of the Bluegrass Case Study is the Inner Bluegrass, approximately 2,400 square miles of gently rolling karst topography with fertile loam soils underlain by calcium-rich limestone, making this one of the most productive agricultural regions in Kentucky. Karst topography is formed from the dissolution of limestone beneath the surface soils. Visually, karst is characterized by gentle uplands and rolling hills dissected by numerous streams and punctuated by spring-fed ponds, sinkholes, limestone outcroppings, natural rock walls, caves, and sinking creeks. The region's creeks and streams are usually shallow and wide with a slow current. All of them drain into one of the two major drainages, the Kentucky River or the Licking River.

The earliest immigrants viewed a Bluegrass much different from today's environment. Two hundred and fifty years ago the area contained a variety of vegetation, including cane breaks, forests, semi-open savanna woodland, and occasional clearings around salt licks. Thickets of cane (*Arundinaria* spp.), the only bamboo native to North America, provided forage for bison and, later, for settler's stock. Due to the ease of clearing by grazing and burning, cane breaks served as the basis of many agricultural fields after settlement.

Deciduous forests covered most of the region before settlement. French botanist F.A. Michaux, while traveling through Kentucky circa 1800, noted forests composed of black cherry, white walnut, buck-eye, ash (white, black, and blue), hackberry, slippery elm, black-jack oak, coffee tree, honey locust, papaw, white oak, sugar maple, beech, plane, yellow poplar, and cucumber tree.

One of the most distinguishing natural features of the Bluegrass is the woodland savanna. Composed of very large, widely spaced deciduous trees (burr oak, white oak, blue ash, and hickory), sparse woody undergrowth, and lush grasses, the woodland savanna is a significant remnant of the presettlement landscape. The park-like conditions of this woodland type were probably maintained by the grazing patterns of bison and the use of fire by Native Americans.

After settlement, many tracts of deciduous forest and woodland savanna were enclosed and utilized as pasturage for livestock. The resulting woodland pasture had the park-like appearance of the woodland savanna yet natural tree regeneration was severely limited due to the intensity of grazing by horses and cattle.

The four distinct periods of history represented in the Bluegrass landscape of today are Exploration and Settlement (1775–1820); the Antebellum Years (1820–1865); the Industrial Age (1866–1918) and; Between the Wars (1919–1945). The major historical themes include exploration and settlement, agriculture, domestic architecture, transportatation, commerce, education, landscape architecture, social and political history, and African-American heritage. Events within the themes of agriculture and transportation have been the major shapers of today's physical environment.

Since settlement in the late 1700s, the region's most valuable resource has been the land itself. Even before the Bluegrass became densely settled in the early 1800s, fertile loam soils underlain by calcium-rich limestone and the abundance of water placed it as one of the most productive agricultural regions in America. In the decades before the Civil War, an agriculture based on the improvement of fine-blooded livestock and the cultivation of hemp, corn, grains, seeds, and grasses placed the Bluegrass in a prominent national position.

Despite the upheavals of the Civil War, agriculture continued to dominate the region's economy for almost another century. Before 1900, the introduction and widespread acceptance of light and burley tobacco as a dependable cash crop and the development of thoroughbred and standardbred horse farms further diversified the agricultural economy and continued to utilize the land as a renewable resource. Signature-styled buildings and maintained pastures, paddocks, fields, and fences characterized the specialized horse farm, while the steeply gabled tobacco barn and silos among extensive fields of ripening leaf tobacco rapidly became typical features of the rural landscape (Figs. 1.10 and 1.11).

Agriculture, commerce, and manufacturing figured importantly in changing the face of the Settlement Period Bluegrass landscape. All of these activities were affected by transportation to greater or lesser degrees. Successful commercial towns were located at ferry crossings, river landings, crossroads, along early rights-of-way, and near salt licks. Salt works at the licks, early distilleries, wagon works, and ship manufacturers, likewise, depended upon adjacent river, stream, or road transportation to export their wares to locations within and outside the Bluegrass.

Settlement roads were often established on buffalo trails or blazed through forests as a simple cleared narrow path that linked two points: a county seat or a major road to a small mill or river landing. The settlement period road system, for the most part, conformed to the natural topography by joining small localities via landscape features such as drainages and ridgelines.

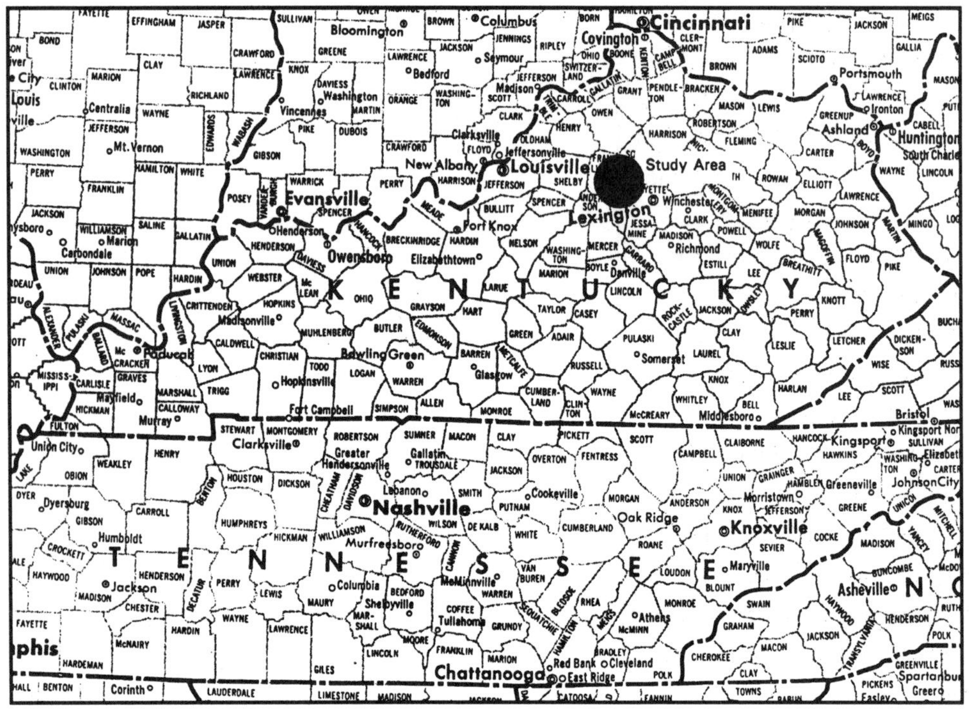

Figure 1.9 *Bluegrass Locator Map.*

Figure 1.10 *Diversified Agriculture.*

The mix of diversified agricultural farms and thoroughbred horse farms contributes to the visual character of the Bluegrass landscape.

Figure 1.11 *Horse Farm.*

During the Antebellum Period, state and local governments and private groups spent large sums to both establish and upgrade land routes. Routes used by drovers to herd stock to distant markets became legitimate national roads linking the state and the central Bluegrass to distant markets. Many of today's highways were established in this way. Within the commonwealth, under the administration of the county courts, a new system of roads linked counties and regions. The new regional network supplanted the earlier network of small local roads.

Lexington's dominant regional role resulted in a primary central Bluegrass transportation pattern that resembled the spokes of a wheel converging on Lexington, the hub. The tangents connected Lexington to the Bluegrass county seats of Versailles, Frankfort, Georgetown, Cynthiana, Paris, Richmond, Nicholasville, Danville, Harrodsburg, and Lancaster, and to points outside the region like Maysville, Louisville, and Cincinnati. Each county, likewise, sent connectors to neighboring seats with a secondary hub and spoke network that mimicked the larger pattern.

That section of the Danville-Lexington-Louisville Road between Lexington and Frankfort, known as Old Frankfort Pike, is one of the finest remaining examples of a primary regional road. In Woodford County there is a four-mile stretch where stone fences and an arched canopy of trees provide the modern day traveler with a distinct historical experience of high integrity. One old toll house still exists at the Nugents Crossroads Community. Primary regional roads such as Old Frankfort Pike that have maintained their historic integrity are considered more rare than their secondary counterparts.

Secondary roads connect sites within communities and, in turn, to the primary routes. These roads are quite narrow (10 to 12 feet wide), often with stone fences on either side. Historically, metal-rimmed wagon wheels cut deeply into the ground on slopes, creating many instances where the roadbed is several feet below the grade of surrounding fields.

Pisgah Pike, in Woodford County, is a good example of a Bluegrass secondary road. Because of modern decline in use, and the continuation of agricultural practices along its borders, this inter-county connector has maintained a high degree of historical integrity. Some of the region's most distinctive osage orange canopies exist along segments of this scenic route.

2

Cultural Features

"It was a pleasant thing to go on a walk with him. The country was to him a living being, developing under his eyes, and the history of its past was to be discovered from the conditions of the present."[6]

This chapter is intended to help users identify and understand cultural features within the rural landscape, so that effective protection measures can be developed and implemented. The chapter also describes a method for preparing a "field guide" to the landscape. The guide is a graphic presentation of landscape characteristics which can be used by the study team to help identify historic resources along the road. It is also an educational document used to enhance public awareness and appreciation of local historic resources which may presently be overlooked.

Landscape Characteristics

Today's rural historic landscapes are the result of cultural processes that have shaped the land over time. To understand the visual character of the region as it currently exists, it is necessary to identify and describe its component parts. The relationship of these components, or *landscape characteristics,* has created the visual patterns that "... reflect human history in the fabric of the land itself."[7]

The National Park Service has described landscape characteristics as "*...the tangible evidence of the activities and habits of the people who occupied, developed, used, and shaped the land to serve human needs; they may reflect the beliefs, attitudes, traditions, and values of these people.*"[8] To help in registering rural historic landscapes on the National Register of Historic Places, the Park Service has identified eleven landscape characteristics:

- Land use and activities
- Patterns of spatial organization
- Response to the natural environment
- Cultural traditions
- Circulation networks
- Boundary demarcations
- Vegetation related to land use
- Buildings, structures, and objects
- Clusters
- Archaeological sites
- Small-scale elements

Definitions of these eleven characteristics are provided below to aid in regional identification. They were taken directly from the National Register of Historic Places Bulletin Number 30 entitled *Guide-*

lines for Evaluating and Documenting Rural Historic Landscapes, by Linda McClelland et al., and *Cultural Landscape: Rural Historic Districts in the National Park System*, by Robert Melnick.

These definitions were developed by the Park Service to help evaluate potential National Register properties. Not all of these characteristics may be applicable to the study area, so the list should only be used as a general guide. Modify or tailor it to suit specific regional conditions. Also, note that example illustrations from the two case studies are in many cases unique to the region; nevertheless, they should provide handbook users with a good idea of the kinds of features to identify.

Land use and activities are the major human forces that shape and organize communities. Activities such as farming, mining, ranching, fishing, recreation, commerce, or industry leave distinct imprints upon the land. Topographic variations, availability of transportation, the abundance or scarcity of natural resources (especially water), cultural traditions, and economic factors influence the ways people use the land. Changing land uses may have resulted from factors ranging from improved technology to climatic changes. Activities visible today may reflect traditional practices or be innovative, yet compatible, adaptations of historic ones (Figs. 2.1 and 2.2).

Patterns of spatial organization are the organization of land on a large scale which depends on a relationship among major physical components, predominant landforms, and natural features. Organization is reflected in road systems, field patterns, distance between farmsteads, proximity to water sources, and orientation of structures to sun and wind. Large-scale patterns characterizing the settlement and early history of an area may remain constant, while individual features, such as buildings and vegetation, change over time (Figs. 2.3 and 2.4).

Response to the natural environment includes major natural features, such as mountains, prairies, rivers, lakes, forests, and grasslands, which influenced both location and organization of communities. Climate, similarly, influenced the siting of buildings, construction materials, and the

Land Use and Activities

Figure 2.1

Red Hills Logging Activity. Mature pines are harvested on the plantations by the single tree selection method. This sustained yield forestry practice and the use of prescribed fires maintains the park-like appearance of the landscape as well as an abundance of quail.

Figure 2.2

Bluegrass Horse Farms. The Kentucky "gentlemen farms" of the Antebellum Period counted horses among their stock. However, 20th century farms that were devoted almost exclusively to raising horses were often "hobby farms" for owners who had made their money in industrial ventures. The investors in the post–Civil War, industrial age horse farms were often new to Kentucky. Today, these farms are not just hobbies but a source of income to their owners.

Patterns of Spatial Organization

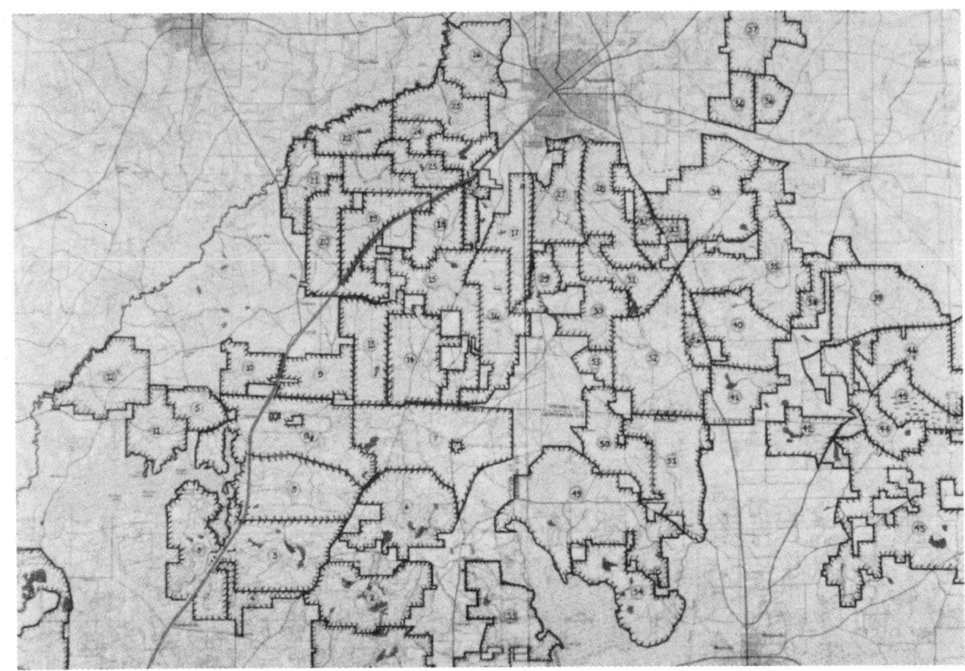

Figure 2.3

Red Hills Ownership Pattern. The large-scale organization of the Red Hills is reflected in the boundaries of the large quail hunting plantations. Today the ownership pattern of large contiguous plantations is very similar to that of the Antebellum Period. Cotton plantations were on average 2,500 acres, compared to the 5,000 acre average of today's quail plantations.

Figure 2.4

Springhouse. The Bluegrass Region's karst topography consists of limestone near the surface of the ground, which dissolves easily and creates springs, sinkholes, and other "karst" features. The sources of pure water were a major influence on the location and organization of the regions earliest rural communities and farmsteads.

Response to the Natural Environment

Figure 2.5

Lake Basin, Red Hills. The red, fertile soils of the uplands and the large shallow lake basins have supported the agricultural activities of man for over 2,000 years.

Figure 2.6

Tilled Soil with Grassy Strip. The fertile loam soils of the Bluegrass strongly influenced the settlement and subsequent agricultural development of the region. Agriculture has been the area's dominant land use throughout history and has shaped the landscape as it appears today.

location of clusters of buildings and structures. Traditions in land use, construction methods, and social customs commonly evolved as people responded to the physiography and ecological systems of the area where they settled (Figs. 2.5 and 2.6).

Cultural traditions have interacted with the natural environment, manipulating and perhaps altering it, and sometimes modifying their traditions in response to it. Cultural traditions determined the structure of communities by influencing the diversity of buildings, location of roads and village centers, and ways the land was worked. Social customs dictated the crops planted or livestock raised. Traditional building forms, methods of construction, stylistic finishes, and functional solutions evolved in the work of local artisans (Figs. 2.7 and 2.8).

Circulation networks are systems for transporting people, goods, and raw materials from one point to another. They range in scale from livestock trails and footpaths, to roads, canals, major highways, and even airstrips. Some, such as farm or lumbering roads, internally served a community, while others, such as railroads and waterways, connected the community to the surrounding region (Figs. 2.9 and 2.10).

Boundary demarcations delineate areas of ownership and land use, such as an entire farmstead or open range. They also separate smaller areas having special functions, such as a fenced field or enclosed corral. Fences, walls, tree lines, hedgerows, drainage or irrigation ditches, roadways, creeks, and rivers commonly mark historic boundaries (Figs. 2.11 and 2.12).

Vegetation related to land use describes various types of vegetation that bear a direct relationship to long-established patterns of land use. Vegetation includes not only crops, trees, or shrubs planted for agricultural and ornamental purposes, but also trees that have grown up incidentally along fence lines, beside roads, or in abandoned fields. Vegetation may include indigenous, naturalized, or introduced species. While many features change over time, vegetation is perhaps the most dynamic. It grows and changes with time,

Cultural Traditions

Figure 2.7

Hunting Dog. For more than a century gamebird hunting, especially of the Bobwhite quail, has provided the basis for the management and appearance of the Red Hills landscape.

Figure 2.8

Horse Racing. This ancient sport spawned the equine industry in the Bluegrass.

Circulation Networks

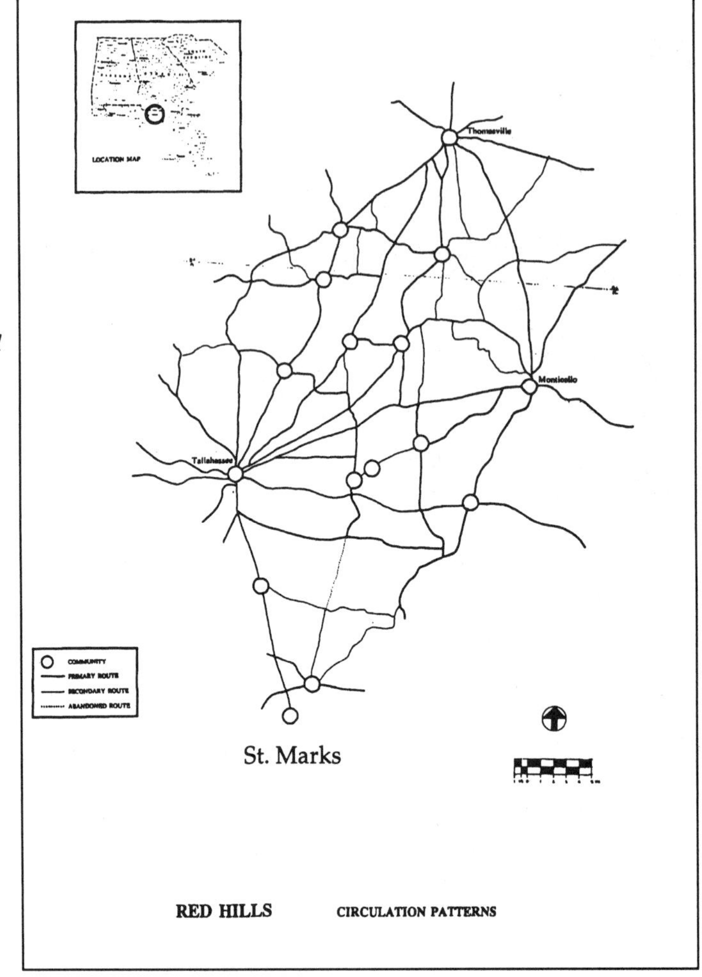

Figure 2.9

Red Hills Radial Transportation Network, circa 1850. Radial networks of roads into Tallahassee reflect the period when Tallahassee was the major market town for cotton. Cotton was hauled to town via ox-drawn wagons and shipped by rail to the port of St. Marks.

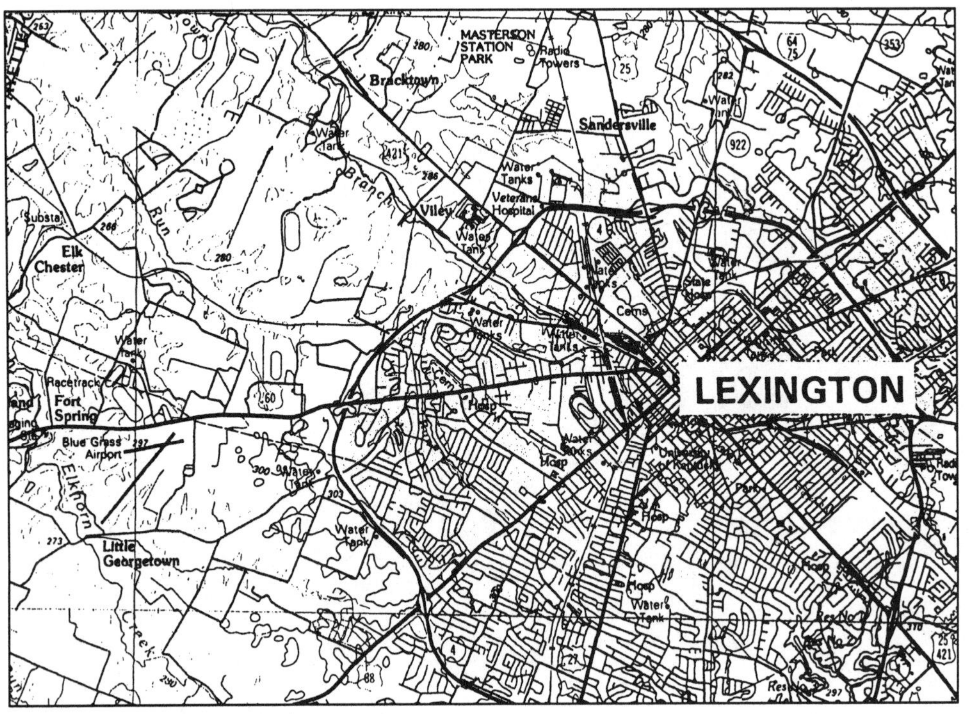

Figure 2.10

Bluegrass Transportation Pattern. Lexington's status as the commercial heart of the central Bluegrass is reflected in the primary transportation network. This historical "hub and spoke" pattern of roads is the result of connectors to neighboring county seats.

Boundary Demarcation

Figure 2.11

Red Hills Firebreak. Because fencing is not commonly employed in the Red Hills, fire breaks often provide the only clue as to the boundary location between two quail plantations.

Figure 2.12

Bluegrass Rock Fence. One of the most identifiable and characteristic boundary markers in the Bluegrass is the rock fence. The oldest rock fences were dry-laid (set with no mortar) in the 1840s by Irish masons who fled the potato famine in Ireland. Rock fences are also mistakenly called "slave fences," in the erroneous belief that plantation slaves constructed them. While slaves assisted the masons by quarrying rock, they were not the builders. After the Civil War, freed slaves began to work as masons and contributed to the rock fences still existing throughout the region.

Vegetation Related to Land Use

Figure 2.13

Red Hills Live Oak Hammock. This upland hardwood forest is a closed-canopy forest of hardwood trees, including the stately live oak. The hammock is found on moist slopes, drainage-ways, and bottomlands where moist soil conditions retard the spread of fire from adjacent upland pine/grassland communities. An alternating pattern of upland pine on the hilltops and hillsides and hardwood stands in the bottomlands and drainages is a persistent visual pattern that exists along roads throughout the Red Hills.

Figure 2.14

Woodland Pasture. Settlers often enclosed tracts of deciduous forest and woodland savanna as pasture for livestock. Trees were selectively cleared, allowing shade for the animals to take shelter during hot summer days. Woodland pastures have a park-like appearance, though natural tree regeneration is severely limited due to the intensity of grazing by horses and cattle. Today, new seedlings are often planted in the pastures and protected by fences, which prevent horses from eating the bark and damaging or killing the young trees.

whether or not people care for it (Figs. 2.13 and 2.14).

Buildings, structures, and objects include various types of these features that serve human needs related to the occupation and use of the land. Their function, materials, date, condition, construction methods, and location reflect the historic activities, customs, tastes, and skills of the people who built and used them. Buildings—designed to shelter human activity—include residences, schools, churches, outbuildings, barns, stores, community halls, and train depots. Structures—designed for functions other than shelter—include dams, canals, systems of fencing, systems of irrigation, tunnels, mining shafts, grain elevators, silos, bridges, earthworks, ships, and highways. Objects—relatively small but important stationary or movable constructions—include markers and monuments, small boats, machinery, and equipment (Figs. 2.15 and 2.16).

Clusters are groupings of buildings, fences, and other features, as seen in a farmstead, ranch, or mining complex, that result from function, social tradition, climate, or other influences, cultural or natural. The arrangement of clusters may reveal information about historical and continuing activities, as well as the impact of varying technologies and preferences of particular generations (Figs. 2.17 and 2.18).

Archaeological sites are sites of prehistoric or historic activities or occupation, which may be marked foundations, ruins, changes in vegetation, and surface remains. They may provide valuable information about the ways the land has been used, patterns of social history, or the methods and extent of activities such as shipping, milling, lumbering, or quarrying. Ruins, changes in vegetation, the spatial distribution of features, surface disturbances, subsurface remains, patterns of soil erosion and deposition, and soil composition may yield information about the evolution and past uses of the land (Figs. 2.19 and 2.20).

Small-scale elements, such as a foot bridge or road sign, add to the historic setting of a landscape. These features may be characteristic of a region and occur repeatedly throughout an area. While most small-scale elements are long-lasting, some, such as bales of hay, are

Buildings, Structures, and Objects

Figure 2.15

Historic Church in the Red Hills. There are numerous churches scattered throughout the Red Hills, many of which serve the small black hamlets in the region. The congregations are, in many cases, descendants of tenant farmers and slaves. Some of the Antebellum Period churches, which were historically attended by all white congregations (some had balconies for slaves) still hold services today. All denominations at one time or another undertook missionary work among black congregations on many of the cotton plantations throughout the region.

Figure 2.16

Bluegrass Tobacco Barn. Tobacco barns need excellent air circulation to allow the tobacco to dry, known as "air-curing." For this reason, the barns are usually built on ridge tops—the long side running east to west—and vented to catch the breeze. Most tobacco in the Bluegrass region today is "burley" tobacco, a light tobacco used in cigarettes. Before burley tobacco, a dark leaf tobacco was raised and smoke-cured.

Clusters

Figure 2.17

Quail Plantation, Red Hills. Associated with each hunting plantation is a complex consisting of the plantation manager's home, barns and other outbuildings, and kennels. These facilities, which support agricultural and hunting operations, are usually located within the interior of the property and not visible to the public. However, a few management complexes at main entrances can usually be seen from public roads. Most structures are wooden framed with tin roofs and painted a uniform color, either dark green or yellow.

Figure 2.18

Agricultural Complex, Bluegrass Region. The relationship of the main residence, barns, sheds, silos, and springhouses on diversified farms create a distinct "cluster" landscape pattern in the region.

Archaeological Sites

Figure 2.19

Antebellum Cotton Plantation Ruins. The ruins of this main residence provides important clues about the activities and lifestyles of the cotton planter and his family.

Figure 2.20

Abandoned Homesite Remains, Bluegrass Region.

VEGETATION RELATED TO LAND USE

Upland Pine Forest

A vegetative community characterized as a rolling, open-canopied forest of pines and scattered hardwoods with few understory shrubs and a dense ground cover of grasses and herbs. Pristine areas are dominated by longleaf pine and wiregrass, while areas that suffered agricultural disturbance are dominated generally by shortleaf and loblolly pines and oldfield grasses and herbs.

Fire is a dominant factor in the ecology of this community because it reduces hardwood encroachment and facilitates the reproduction of pine and herbaceous plants. Without relatively frequent fires, upland pine forest succeeds to upland mixed forest and eventually to upland hardwood forest. While lightning has served as an important ignition source for fire throughout

Red Hills

A FIELD GUIDE TO THE HISTORIC BLUEGRASS LANDSCAPE

Land Uses and Related Vegetation

Savanna Woodland

One of the most distinguishing natural features of the Bluegrass is the woodland savanna. Composed of very large, widely spaced deciduous trees (burr oak, white oak, blue ash, and hickory), sparse woody undergrowth and lush grasses, the woodland savanna is a significant remnant of the pre-settlement landscape. The parklike conditions of this woodland type were probably maintained by the grazing patterns of bison and the use of fire by native Americans.

Woodland Pastures

After settlement many tracts of deciduous forest and woodland savanna were enclosed and utilized as pasturage for livestock. Trees were selectively cleared so that there would still be shade for the animals to take shelter during hot summer days. Woodland pastures have the parklike appearance of the woodland savanna yet natural tree regeneration is severely limited due to the intensity of grazing by horses and cattle. Today, you'll often see new seedlings planted in the pastures and fenced to protect the young trees from horses which eat the bark and damage or kill the trees.

Bluegrass

Figure 2.23 *Sample Sheets from the Red Hills and Bluegrass Field Guides.*

Landscape Characteristics, By Era, Of the Red Hills Region

	Early Pre-History 10,000 B.C. - 0	Late Pre-History 0 – 1550	Spanish Contact 1550 – 1700	Colonial Period 1700 – 1820	Antebellum Period 1820 – 1865	Reconstruction 1865 – 1900	Early 20th Century 1900 – 1920	Late 20th Century 1920 – Present
Cultural Traditions	Hunting/gathering Nomadic Temporary Settlements	Hunting/Gathering Agriculture/ Horticulture Permanent Settlements	Agriculture Conversion to Christianity Spanish Language/Culture	Hunting/Gathering Agriculture European Influence on Natives	White Planting Culture Agriculture Dependant on Slave System	Tenant System of Agriculture Planters Become Landlords	Wealthy/Leisure Class Becomes Predominant Black Tenants Work Quail Plantations Small Farmers (500 Acres and Less)	Wealthy Northern Families Winter Quail Plantations Blacks Leave Plantations
Land Use and Activities	Hunting/Gathering Dependance on Wildlife Use of Fire	Extensive Corn Culture System of Fields Use of Fire	Extensive Corn Culture Livestock Raising New Crops/Animals	More Diverse Crops Extensive Use of Livestock	Extensive Cotton/Corn Culture Extensive Use of Livestock Apalachee Indian Oldfield Sites	Extensive Cotton/Corn Culture Extensive Use of Livestock Patch Farming Use of Fire	Patch Farming Small Grain Fields Quail Hunting Small Farmers Diversify	Patch Farming Small Grain Fields Quail Hunting Forestry/Fire Management
Organizational Patterns	Based on Natural Resources Temporary Settlements Near Water	Satellite Villages Individual Farmstead Large Field Sizes Mound Sites Settlements Near Areas w/ Good Soils	Mission Site Settlements Extensive Fields East-West Orientations Haciendas	Seminole Villages in and Around Large Lake Basins Field Sizes Unknown Use of Apalachee Indian Oldfield Sites	Large Ownerships Large Fields Interspersed with Woodlots Township/Range Used in Florida; Metes/Bounds in Georgia	Large Ownerships Remain Intact Field Size Shrinks (40 Acres) Field Patchwork	Large Ownerships Field Patchwork Maintained by Agricultural Practices	Large Ownerships Field Patchwork Maintained by Agricultural and Fire Management Practices
Response to Natural Environment	Based on Natural Resources Settlements Near Water	Permanent Settlements Near Water and Uplands with Good Soils	Good Soils Determine Agricultural Activities Hilltop Mission Sites Near Apalachee Indian Villages	Seminole Villages in and Around Large Lake Basins	Cotton Fields Based on Soil Conditions Locations Relative to Large Lake Basins Use of Apalachee Indian/Spanish Oldfield Sites	Agricultural Fields Based on Soil Conditions Use of Meadows/Grasslands near Large Lake Basins for Grazing	Hunting Lodges Located on Hillsides Overlooking Lakes	Hunting Lodges Located on Hillsides Overlooking Lakes Fire Management Results in Pine Parkland on Upland and Hardwood Stands Along Drainages

Figure 2.24 *Historical Landscape Matrix.*

Landscape Characteristics, By Era, Of the Red Hills Region

	Early Pre-History 10,000 B.C. - 0	Late Pre-History 0 – 1550	Spanish Contact 1550 – 1700	Colonial Period 1700 – 1820	Antebellum Period 1820 – 1865	Reconstruction 1865 – 1900	Early 20th Century 1900 – 1920	Late 20th Century 1920 – Present
Vegetation Related to Land Use	Longleaf Pine Matrix Hardwoods in Bottomland and Drainages	Extensive Cropland-Corn, Beans, Squash Longleaf Pine- Pine Parkland Hardwoods in Bottomland and Drainages	Extensive Cropland, Especially near Mission Sites Spanish Introduce Diversity of Crops and Livestock	Extensive Agriculture Woodland Pasture Forested Lands	Extensive Agriculture (Corn, Cotton) Woodlots Early Successional Vegetation on Depleted Fields	Agricultural Diversity (Fruits and Vegetables) Particularly in Leon County Oldfield Pine Regeneration Patchy Network of Hedgerows	Small Farms - Agricultural Diversity (Fruits, Vegetables) Small Corn and Grain Plots Abandoned Fields of Broomsedge	Mosaic of Small Grain Fields Corn, Millet within Oldfield Pine Stands Longleaf Pine Stands
Boundary Demarcations	Based on Natural Waterbody Features- Rivers, Lakes, Marshes	Based on Natural Waterbody Features- Rivers, Lakes, Marshes Field Edges	Based on Natural Waterbody Features- Rivers, Lakes, Marshes Field Edges	Based on Natural Waterbody Features- Rivers, Lakes, Marshes Field Edges	Fencing, Roads, Railroads Fencerow/Hedgerow Woodlots	Fencing, Roads, Railroads Fencerows/Hedgerows Woodlots Field Edges	Roads, Roadside Vegetation Fencing not Prominent Wood Edges Hedgerows	Roads, Roadside Vegetation Fencing not Prominent Firebreaks Hedgerows
Structures And Objects	Temporary Wooden Shelters	Mound Sites Wooden Structures	Mission Sites, Including Churches, Convents, Spanish and Indian Houses, Fort, Plaza, Council Houses	Seminole Village Sites Indian Houses Town Square	Antebellum Homes Slave Quarters Cemeteries Stores	Antebellum Homes Cemeteries Tenant Structures Stores	Hunting Lodges Horse Stables Private Bridges Plantation Entrances Barns, Sheds, Kennels	Plantation Signs Wrought Iron Gates Posted Security Signs
Archaeological Sites	Indian Village Sites	Mound Sites Village Sites	Mission Sites	Seminole Villages	Plantation Complex	Tenant Homes Farm Complex		

Figure 2.24 (*continued*)

Landscape Characteristics, By Era, Of the Red Hills Region

	Early Pre-History 10,000 B.C. - 0	Late Pre-History 0 – 1550	Spanish Contact 1550 – 1700	Colonial Period 1700 – 1820	Antebellum Period 1820 – 1865	Reconstruction 1865 – 1900	Early 20th Century 1900 – 1920	Late 20th Century 1920 – Present
Clusters	Indian Village Sites	Mound Sites Satellite Village Sites Individual Farmsteads	Mission Sites Village Sites	Seminole Villages	Plantation Complex Community Clusters Crossroads w/ Store	Community Clusters with Dwellings and Churches Plantation Complex Crossroads w/ Store	Hunting Lodge and Outbuildings Managers's Residence and Outbuildings Residential Clusters with Church Crossroads Store Disappears	Hunting Lodge and Outbuildings Managers's Residence and Outbuildings Residential Clusters with Church Crossroads Store Disappears
Circulation Networks	Trail System Linking Temporary Village Sites	Trail System Linking Permanent Village Sites - Heavy use into Interior of Sites	Trail System with East/West Road Linking Apalachee/St. Augustine Missions	Well-Established Trail System Between Villages	Roads Formed from Old Trails as Result of Cotton Wagons East/West Railroad System	Interior Plantation Network Forms East/West Railroad System and North/South Linkage	Chain Gangs Maintain Road System Interior Plantation Circulation Related to Shooting Course	Paving with Automobile Use Diverse Road Types
Trail/Road Structure	Trails/Footpaths Providing Access to Natural Resources	Trails/Footpaths Providing Access to Natural Resources/Agricultural Areas Trading Routes Form	Trails Verging on Roads Form From Use by Carts and Wagons	Well-Established Trails/Roads Providing Access to Natural Resource and Agricultural Areas	Canopy Roads Cut Banks	Canopy Roads, Cut Banks Slave Labor Maintenance Road Improvements	Prison Labor Maintenance Road Improvement - Paving Roads Lose Social Importance	Road Improvement Diversity of Road Types Roads Lose Social Importance

Figure 2.24 (*continued*)

the study team to quickly determine how each historic period is presently represented in the landscape. Information collected in the matrix was used to prepare an interpretive tour guide to the region, with which users could discover historical regional details era by era, as if "travelling through time."

Questions to Ask

How should the landscape characteristics be described in the field guide?

Which illustrations best represent each characteristic?

If prepared as an educational document, where should the field guide be distributed?

How could a landscape matrix be used?

Is there enough information about the historic periods of the region to construct a landscpae matrix?

3

THE VISUAL EXPERIENCE

"Viewed solely as an amenity, scenery is too often replaced by … technological achievement(s). Viewed as an essential bond between people and their surroundings, a scenic environment has no substitution." [9]

In the previous chapter, landscape characteristics were looked at solely from the standpoint of historical resources. This chapter adds another layer—the visual resource. In rural historic landscapes, visual resources are shaped for the most part by historic circumstances and activities such as settlement patterns, land uses, and land management practices. A region's landscape offers a visual record of its history, reflecting generational beliefs and traditions.

It is important to distinguish between *scenic* and *visual* resources. Though related, they are not synonymous, for it is the valuation of the visual resources through public preference and consensus that defines its scenic quality. Scenic resources reflect shared images of what is special or unique about a region's landscape, and establishing these collective community values is essential to ultimately making sound protection decisions. This chapter describes a community-based participation process for determining scenic resources, in which local residents help define and identify their most preferred landscapes.

Public road corridors are important visual resources because they are the places *where most people experience rural landscapes most of the time.* (This handbook distinguishes between "roadway" and "road corridor." "Roadway" is that area of the public right-of-way, while "road corridor" includes both the right-of-way and the visible landscape on either side.) The sequence of visual images along corridors influences the way people perceive the larger landscape. Visual experiences along road corridors are resources which should be classified and evaluated so that measures can be devised to protect, enhance, and restore significant scenic qualities.

Described on the following pages is a method for determining the scenic significance of visually distinct landscape types, which was applied in the Red Hills to determine which road types within the regional network were most preferred. The focus in the Red Hills Case Study was on the travel experience along the immediate *roadway*. The Bluegrass Case Study, on the other hand, involved only two

"The method for determining scenic value should be a defensible one if we hope it will affect the decisions of policy makers."[10]

roads, so the goal was slightly different—to find out which visually distinct landscape types within the two *road corridors* were most preferred in terms of views from the road.

This method of determining the public's visual preferences for distinct landscape types was adapted from studies by Schauman (1987) and The Soil Conservation Service (1985). This approach relies on the opinion of the people who live and work in the region. It adjusts professional judgment by using the local residents' perspectives for determining inherent scenic features. This method assumes that local actions and solutions that are participatory can be powerful forces in protecting and restoring environments.

The determination of scenic resources can be broken down into three basic steps, each with several distinct tasks. The time frame to complete each task will be discussed below, but keep in mind that these estimates are based on conditions in the two case study areas and may have to be modified depending on the situation. The steps are:

1. Define Visual Resources
   - *Identify visually distinct landscape types*
   - *Photograph visually distinct landscape types*
   - *Map visually distinct landscape types*

2. Organize Community Input
   - *Assemble a Scenic Advisory Panel and conduct first meeting*
   - *Simulate visually distinct landscape types, as approved by the Scenic Advisory Panel*
   - *Conduct second Scenic Advisory Panel meeting*

3. Determine Scenically Significant Resources
   - *Conduct visual preference survey*
   - *Analyze and interpret survey results*

Obviously, the assembly of the team that will conduct this study depends on the needs of the group or organization that is sponsoring the work. The skills required of the study team to prepare and conduct the visual preference survey are not difficult, and interested and informed laypersons should have no trouble. As mentioned in the Introduction, however, it may be wise to enlist help from a professional who is knowledgeable in large-scale landscape planning and design issues and comfortable with the concept of "visually distinct landscape types." Landscape architects, environmental planners, or geographers may be helpful. Also, contact the local Soil Conservation Service office for information about the SCS countryside landscape assessment methodology and possible technical assistance.

☞ *While one of the major benefits of working with a professional is time savings, plan on spending at least two or three months on this work even with expert guidance.*

Define Visual Resources

Deciding "where to look" and "what to look for" sounds simple, but these key first steps in defining visual resources must be carefully evaluated. In a large study area with many types of roads, the evaluation may focus more on the roadway instead of the adjacent landscape ("where to look"), and the conditions or attributes of just the roadway instead of the entire road corridor ("what to look for"). If the study area is smaller, more of the adjacent landscape patterns may be included. Regardless of scope, however, there are three main tasks to defining visual resources: identification, photography, and mapping of visually distinct landscape types.

Identify Visually Distinct Landscape Types

Drive the roads in the study area and look for repeated visual patterns along the roadway—road surfaces, verges, ditches, embankments, structures such as fences or utility lines, and vegetation. In the adjacent landscape look for repeated patterns of land uses and vegetation such as cropland, pasture, forest, or wetland. If a field guide was prepared as described in the previous chapter, use it as an aid for identifying different types of roads and landscapes.

During this identification stage, it is helpful to take notes to record the visually distinct patterns. Use only a few descriptors: *narrow tunnel, enclosed view; wide and straight, long views;* and *winding, roller*

There are three main tasks to Step 1: identifying, photographing, and mapping visually distinct units of the landscape that are visible from the public roads in the study area.

Keep in mind that at this stage of information collection, quantity is more important than quality.

coaster, short views are examples for the roadway. *Young pine forest, screened views; cropland, long expansive views;* and *rolling pasture, medium to short views* are alternatives for the adjacent landscape.

Questions to Ask

Given the number of roads in the study area, should the scenic assessment focus on the immediate roadways or include the entire corridor?

What are the different land use types and management practices in the region, and how do they affect the visual character of the landscape?

What are the conditions of the immediate roadway?

How do roadside vegetation and structures affect the visual experience of the travel?

What succinct words or phrases best describe the different distinct visual experiences?

Photograph Visually Distinct Landscape Types

After becoming familiar with the visually distinct landscape types in the study area, photograph them. Remember, at this stage, quantity is more important than quality. Don't get bogged down by paying undue attention to photographic conditions or equipment, for these photos are intended to document the landscape types in preparation for community input. Use a consistent film type—either color or black and white (35 mm color slides are recommended because of their suitability for presentations). Choose viewpoints along the road that provide good representative samples of each landscape type.

Questions to Ask

What scenes best represent the visually distinct landscape types described in the previous step?

Are there any unresolved or confusing landscape patterns?

Where are the best viewpoints for photographing each landscape type?

What type of camera and film is best to use?

Map Visually Distinct Landscape Types

Once the study team has identified and photographed the visually distinct units, they should be mapped (Fig. 3.1). Choosing the most appropriate map and scale is very important and depends on the size of the study area and/or the number and length of roads, and the physiographic characteristics of the region. If, for example, the study area encompasses a two or three county area with two hundred miles of roads, a 1:100,000 scale (1 inch = 1.5 miles) U.S. Geological Survey (USGS) topographic map may be the best bet. For a single ten-mile stretch of road, a USGS 1:24,000 scale (1 inch = 2000 feet) topographical map may be the best choice. Other good base maps are the county highway maps that are published for most states by departments of transportation and often available from county road departments. These vary in scale from one inch per mile to one inch per two miles. Consult the local photocopy or blueprint shop for advice on reducing or enlarging base maps to accommodate the study area.

Maps can be obtained from a variety of sources. Check the yellow pages for private map dealers. Public agencies include the local road department or state department of transportation, the local tax assessor's office, local planning office, and libraries. USGS topographical maps and catalogues can be obtained by mail by contacting the Eastern Mapping Center. (Refer to Appendix E for sources of technical information.)

While there is a lot of flexibility in delineating the visually distinct units on the map, it is probably best to stick to simple, clear patterns, symbols, and lines (Fig. 3.1).

Questions to Ask

Where can base maps be obtained?

What is the best scale to use for preparing the base map?

What symbols, patterns, and colors should be used to delineate the visually distinct landscape types on the base map?

☞ *The time necessary to complete Step 1 will vary with the size of the study area and the number of roads. At a minimum, allow one to two weeks to complete this part of the study.*

Choosing the most appropriate map and scale is for the most part determined by two factors: (1) the size of the study area, and (2) the physiographic characteristics of the region.

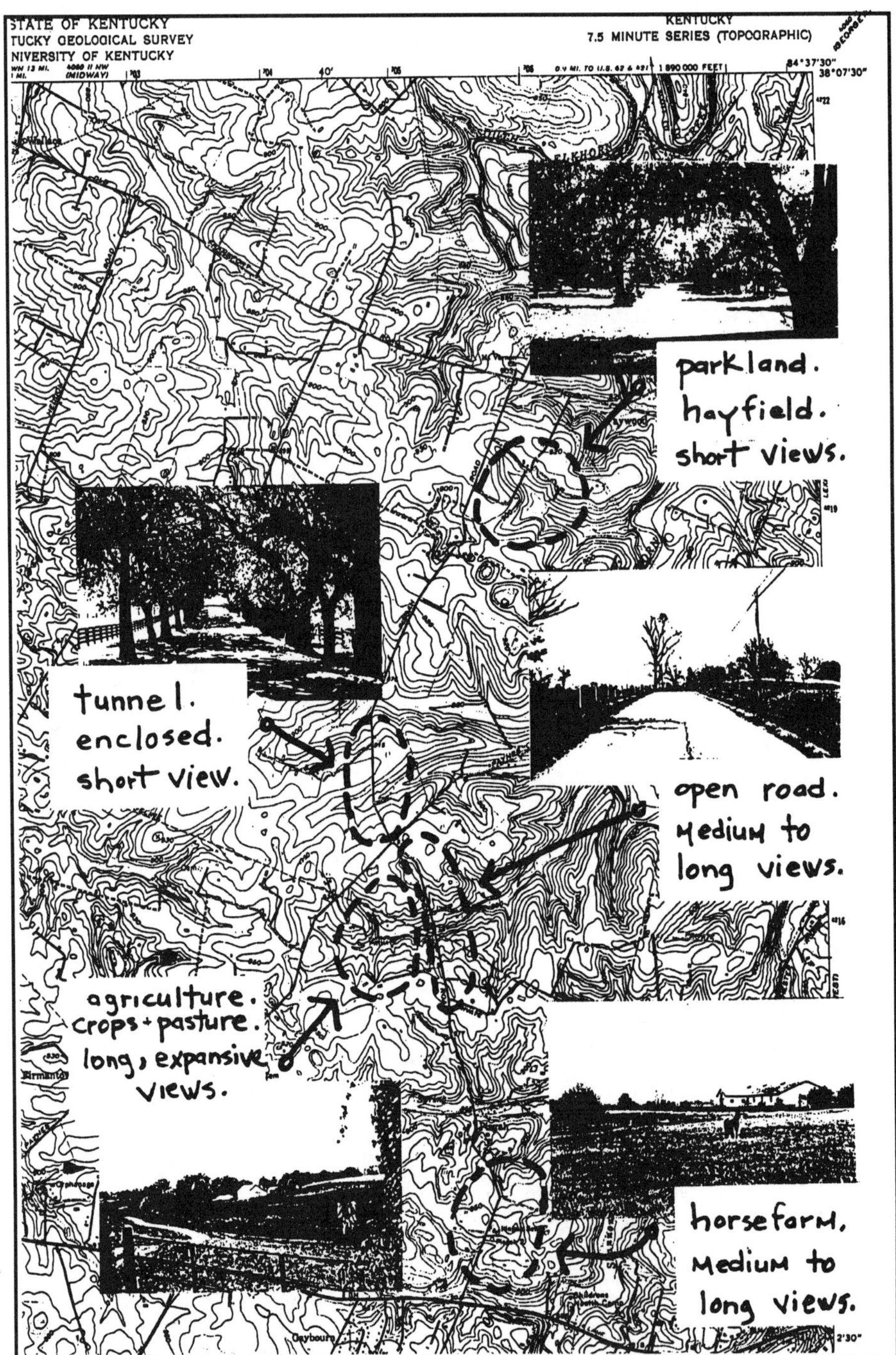

Figure 3.1
Base Map, with Photos and Descriptors.

Red Hills Case Study

The goal in the Red Hills was to define the visually distinct travel experiences along two hundred miles of roads. The descriptors "open," "patchy," and "enclosed" were chosen to describe the visual experiences. Keep in mind that what is considered an "open" experience in the Red Hills could very well be an "enclosed" experience elsewhere. "Open" in this context is defined by long views down the road corridor. "Enclosed" is characterized by the regular pattern of mature trees growing near the road, which creates a tunnel effect. A "patchy" experience is more difficult to define. It is the gray area, not consistently open or enclosed. Patchy could be an enclosed experience evolving into an open experience by the frequent interruption of driveways, development, or pastures (Fig. 3.2).

Bluegrass Case Study

In the Bluegrass there were only two roads in the study area, so the goal was somewhat different than for the Red Hills study. Here, visually disinct units were also defined for road types, but the emphasis was on adjacent landscapes. Visual experiences were described by the study team as "woodland savanna," "thoroughbred horse farm," "diversified agriculture," "residential community," "enclosed road corridor," "open road corridor," "feature view," and "combined/transitional." "Combined/transitional" was a catch-all for what didn't fit neatly into the other units. Such units are difficult to categorize and even more difficult to photograph.

Organize Community Input

Assembling a "Scenic Advisory Panel" of community residents and conducting periodic meetings is critical in determining a study area's scenic resources. The Scenic Advisory Panel members serve as local experts to gauge the efforts of the study team. Ultimately, they verify the integrity of the study team's definitions and representations of the visually distinct landscape types and modify them if necessary. At least two meetings with the

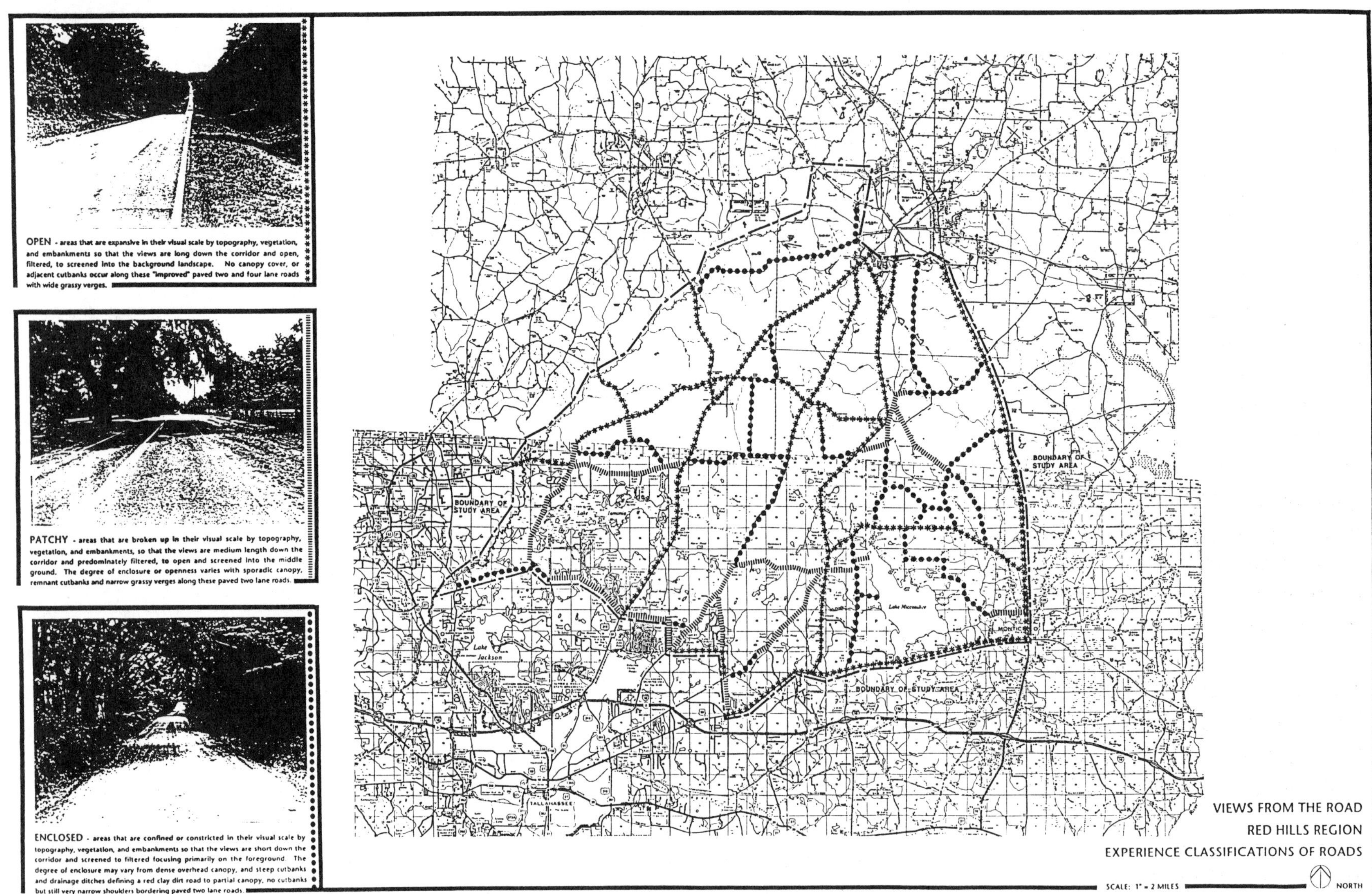

Figure 3.2 *Visually Distinct Road Types in the Red Hills.*

panel are usually needed to accomplish the objectives of this part of the study.

Assemble a Scenic Advisory Panel and Conduct First Meeting

The Scenic Advisory Panel must represent a cross section of the community. Try to invite representatives from as many interest groups as possible to participate, but keep in mind that it is easier to manage 10–20 people than 30–40 people. It is important that the attendees have a good knowledge of the region's roads and landscapes, because they will be asked to map landscape types from memory. Sample letters of invitation that were used for the case studies are provided in Appendix A.

During the first panel meeting, the Scenic Advisory Panel will duplicate from memory the study team's exercise of mapping visually distinct units. They are asked to rely on their memory of the region because the study team must ascertain local perceptions and interpretations of the landscape. This mapping exercise is based on the assumption that the panel members know the local landscape well enough to map it. If not, it may be necessary to conduct a tour of the study area. Panel members may choose to work individually or in teams on clean base maps provided by the study team. Once these maps are completed, the study team should reveal their preliminary photographs and compare maps. Note the differences, and modify the study team maps to reflect the perceptions and consensus of the Scenic Advisory Panel.

☞*Allow a minimum of three hours for the first meeting.*

Questions to Ask

Which community interest groups should be invited to particapte on the Scenic Advisory Panel?

Do the interest groups represent a cross section of the community?

Who is the best representative of each group?

How familiar are potential participants with the region's landscape and its roads?

How should the letter of invitation be worded?

Where should the Scenic Advisory Panel meetings be held?

Ten to twenty representatives of the local community are a manageable size to serve on the panel.

What graphic supplies and other materials will the study team need to conduct the meeting?

Simulate Visually Distinct Landscape Types

After the landscape types have been modified and approved by the Scenic Advisory Panel, they must be simulated through photography or videography. (Obviously, time constraints, budget, personnel, and study goals must be factored into which method to use. For this handbook's two case studies, video worked best in the Red Hills, while photographs were more appropriate for documenting the landscape types in the Bluegrass case study.) Whichever method is used, try to be consistent. Unlike the initial photographic work to document landscape types, quality and consistency are important here, because these simulations will ultimately be used for the visual preference survey that will be administered to the public. (Refer to Appendix B for photographic standards.)

☞*At a minimum, the study team should try to obtain five or six simulations of each landscape type.*

Questions to Ask

How would you best simulate the visually distinct units agreed upon by the Scenic Advisory Panel (still photos vs. video)?

When you have finished, do you have four or five photographic simulations adequately representing each landscape type?

Conduct Second Scenic Advisory Panel Meeting

As soon as possible after the study team has simulated landscape types, conduct the second scenic advisory panel meeting. At the second meeting, the Panel will decide whether or not the simulations represent the agreed upon landscape types. Use a questionnaire to determine this. Number each simulation, show it to the Panel and have them indicate on the questionnaire which landscape type they think the simulation represents.

☞*As a general rule, the completion of the questionnaire should not take more than twenty or thirty minutes. An example of the landscape classification questionnaires used in the case study areas can be found in Appendix C.*

Next, have the study team analyze the completed questionnaires to determine which simulations reliably represent the landscape types. *A simulation can be considered representative if more than half of the panelists voted for it.*

Although percentages are easily calculated using a pocket calculator, there are also easy-to-use statistical programs available for personal computers which can significantly shorten calculation time. An added benefit of some programs is their ability to construct bar graphs and charts which facilitate the quick visual analysis of questionnaire results (Fig. 3.3).

Questions to Ask

How would you determine Scenic Advisory Panel consensus on simulations which represent landscape types?

What computer software is available for conducting simple statistical analysis of the questionnaire results?

After analyzing the landscape classification questionnaire, do you have three or four approved simulations of each landscape type?

Red Hills Case Study

For the Red Hills region, there were twelve Scenic Advisory Panel members recommended by the Red Hills Conservation Association. These citizens from the local community represented the following interests:

- Plantation owners
- Plantation managers
- Foresters
- Biologists
- Historic preservationists
- Small farmers
- Residents of small communities within the region
- Local elected officials

At the first Scenic Advisory Panel meeting, the panel approved the three travel experiences as preliminarily defined by the study team and worked in teams of two to map "open," "enclosed," and "patchy" landscape types. (Refer to Fig. 3.2.)

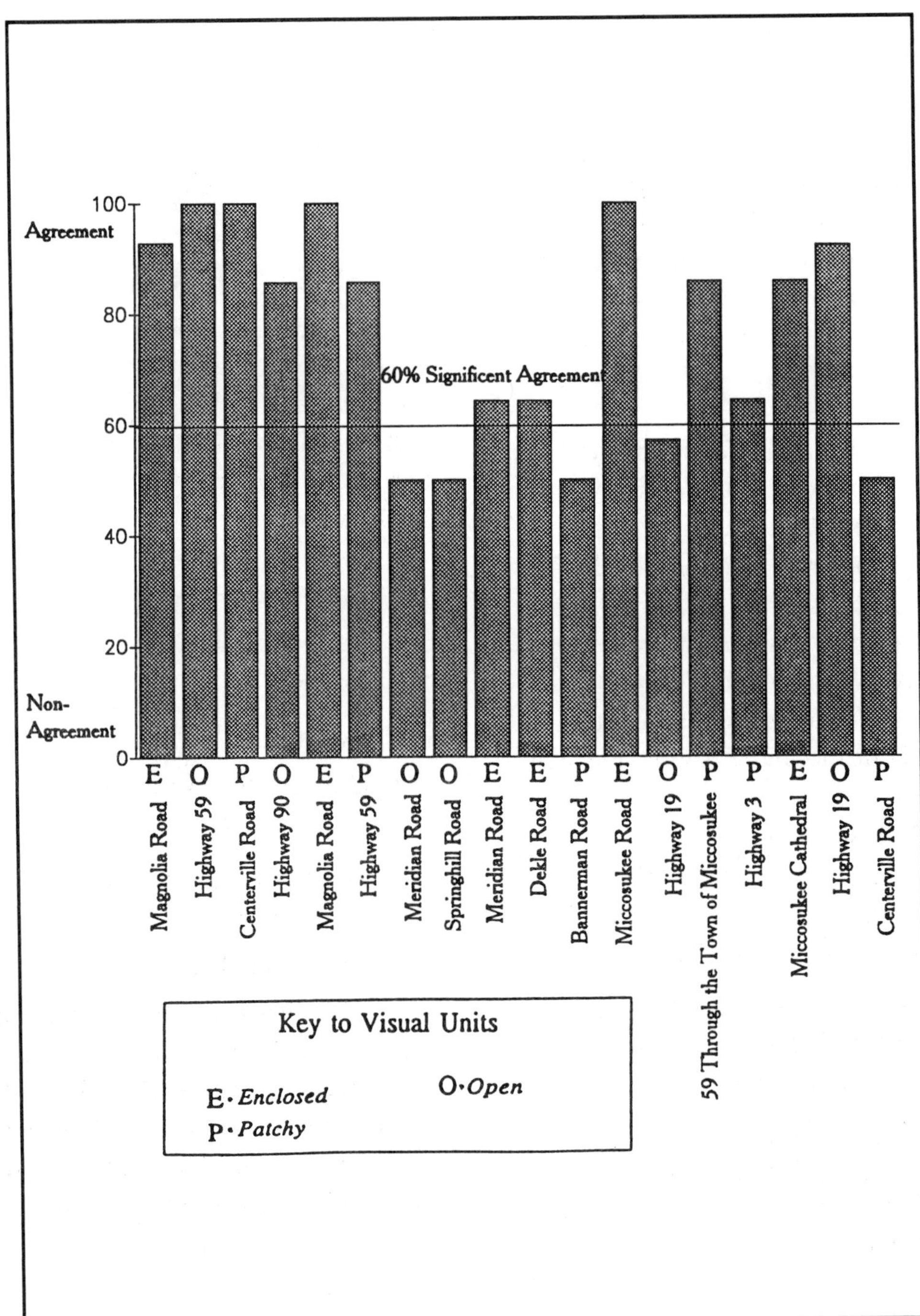

Figure 3.3
Graphic Summary of Responses for Visually Distinct Landscape Types in the Red Hills.

The study team videotaped, throughout the study area, six (five minute) segments of each of the three travel experiences, for a total of eighteen video segments. These segments were edited into a random order of one-minute selections of each travel experience.

At the second Scenic Advisory Panel meeting, the panel was asked to classify on a questionnaire each of the eighteen video segments as to one of the three agreed upon landscape types. Consensus was determined by calculating the percentage of votes each simulation received. Video segments which obtained a consensus rating were used as the basis for the public visual preference survey (Fig. 3.3).

Bluegrass Case Study

Slides representing the visually distinct units (as perceived by the study team) were presented to the Scenic Advisory Panel. Clarification about patterns and discrepancies among landscape types were resolved through a discussion over the slides. The panel modified the preliminary landscape types. Initially, the study team recognized "thoroughbred horse farms" as only one landscape type, but the Scenic Advisory Panel educated them as to the different types of horse farming. Ultimately, two distinct types of horse farms were approved by the panel: traditional thoroughbred horse farms and modern thoroughbred horse farms. The other seven landscape types approved by the panel included: diversified agriculture; mixed use (thoroughbred horse farm and diversified agriculture); crossroads community; piano key development; woodland savanna; open road corridor; and enclosed road corridor (Fig. 3.4).

Next, the study team and panel needed to agree on the location of the landscape types along the two study roads. The panel accomplished this by working in teams to delineate with colors the location of landscape types. The panel maps were later used as a guide by the study team as they photographed variations of each landscape type throughout the study area.

At the second meeting, photographs of the landscape types were shown to the panel and they were asked to classify each one. Photos which were agreed upon as

Because this handbook is aimed at assessing views from the public road network, it is imperative that Step 3 provide a means for reflecting public values.

Thoroughbred Horse Farm (modern).

Diversified Agriculture.

Thoroughbred Horse Farm (traditional).

Mixed Use (diversified agriculture and thoroughbred horse farm).

Figure 3.4 *Visually Distinct Landscape Types Agreed Upon by Scenic Advisory Panel, Bluegrass Region.*

Crossroads Community.

Open Road Corridor.

Enclosed Road Corridor.

Woodland Savanna.

Piano Key Development.

Figure 3.4 (*continued*)

representative of the landscape types were used as the basis for the public visual preference survey.

Determine Scenically Significant Resources

This step is to determine which visually distinct landscape types the public prefers. "Public" in this context refers to the people who live and work in the study area. The two main tasks are *to conduct the visual preference survey* by administering a questionnaire and *analyze and interpret the survey results* to determine scenic resources.

Conduct Visual Preference Survey

The visual preference survey is based on a questionnaire which is administered to a representative cross section of the community. Potential survey candidates include members of community groups such as neighborhood associations and garden clubs, business organizations, churches, and schools. Draw on the expertise of the Scenic Advisory Panel in recommending survey respondents.

It is important that the respondents represent the study area population, and that their responses can be generalized to the entire population. Collect demographic data such as age, gender, ethnicity, income, and education from the respondents through a questionnaire administered with the visual preference questionnaire, and compare it (in the next step) with the most current census data for the area under study (see Appendix D).

Show participants photographs or video segments depicting each approved landscape type, and ask them to indicate on the questionnaire the degree to which they like or dislike each scene (where 1 = totally dislike and 5 = like very much—see Appendix D). The images that are used for the survey are the same ones that the Scenic Advisory Panel agreed were representative of the landscape types (described in Step 2). Ideally, there should be three or four simulations representing variations of each landscape type.

☞ *For a valid survey sample, try to obtain at least 150 to 200 responses, which should provide a fair representation of the community. Plan on spending at least a month for administering the survey.*

There are no hard and fast rules for administering the visual preference test or setting the amount of time allowed for viewing each image. Generally, the test should last no longer than ten or fifteen minutes—more than that and people may begin to get restless. Assuming there are twenty to thirty images, allot approximately thirty seconds for the assessment of each image. The goal should be to provide enough time to obtain good first impressions of preference. Don't allow too much time though, for participants may "over-analyze" the images.

Questions to Ask

How would you design the visual preference survey questionnaire?

How much time should be alloted for administering the survey?

How much time should be alloted for assessing each image?

Who will the survey be administered to?

Analyze and Interpret Results

At this stage the study team must analyze the questionnaire results to determine both demographic characteristics of the respondents and their preferred landscape types. The most common statistical measurements for analyzing preferences are the mean, median, and mode. The mean is an average score. It is calculated by adding the scores for each image and dividing the sum by the number of respondents. The median is the middle number, the value that exactly divides the group of responses in half. The mode is the most frequent answer, the most common value among responses to an item. The choice of which measurement, or combination of measurements, to use for analyzing the results of the surveys depends on the pattern, or range, of scores.

In both case studies the pattern of scores for the visual preference questionnaires was such that the mean (average) scores were adequate for establishing visual preference. Scores can be calculated by breaking them into several preference categories, such as "dislike," "neither like nor dislike," and "like," or simply ranking them from highest to lowest (if the goal is to determine only the most preferred landscape type). Keep in mind that a wide spread of scores may require additional statistical measures. If help is needed in conducting a more thorough statistical analysis, contact an expert such as a statistician, economist, social scientist, planner, or geographer.

A good way to compare measures is to graph them. Bar graphs work well because they clearly depict which images are the most preferred and allow for a quick classification of the images as high, medium, or low preference.

Questions to Ask

What statistical measurement(s) should be used to determine visual preference for landscape types?

If help is needed for a statistical analysis, which local experts might be contacted?

Do the survey respondents represent the community at large?

Red Hills Case Study

In the Red Hills, the goal was to determine the most visually preferred road types. Survey responses were obtained from our outreach to local churches, civic groups, and business organizations. We drew on the regional expertise of the Scenic Advisory Panel to help target groups to survey. At the Scenic Advisory Panel meetings a contact sheet was passed around on which panelists listed the names of organizations and contact people.

The groups were given very little information before testing to insure that the responses were not biased in any way. The test consisted of showing a ten-minute video tape of eighteen, thirty-second road segments representing the approved "open," "patchy," and "enclosed" landscape types. The respondents were asked to indicate on a questionnaire the degree to which they liked or disliked each road segment on a scale of one to five. After the completed questionnaires were collected, the study team described to the group the purpose of the project in more detail and how the results would be used. Questions about the survey were also answered at this time.

The bar graph in Figure 3.5 illustrates the mean (average) score for each video image. It is readily apparent from the graph that the enclosed road segments are the most visually preferred type of travel experience.

Bluegrass Case Study

The questionnaire tested for the visual preference of visually distinct landscape types by showing the local residents the thirty-one photographs that were determined, in Step 2, to be representative samples of eight landscape types. The questionnaire asked the respondents to simply indicate the degree to which they liked or disliked each scene, for whatever reasons (see Appendix D).

The results of the visual preference survey were statistically analyzed by looking at mean scores. The mean is an average score calculated by adding the numbers together and dividing by the number of figures in the set. The Bluegrass bar graph in Figure 3.6a illustrates the mean scores for "likability" for each of the thirty-one photographs used in the survey.

The pattern of scores in the graph in Figure 3.6a suggested that the photographs could be divided into three preference categories. It was determined by the study team that the highest preference category (#1) should include those scenes with a mean score above four. Scenes with a mean score from three to four were placed in the medium preference category (#2). Scenes which received a mean score of less than three were placed in the lowest preference category (#3). Figure 3.6b lists the preference category and landscape type for each of the thirty-one photographs used in the visual preference survey.

Generally, the most preferred landscape types in the Bluegrass study area are the thoroughbred horse farm, enclosed road segment, and woodland savanna. Diversified agriculture and crossroads communities received medium scores most of the

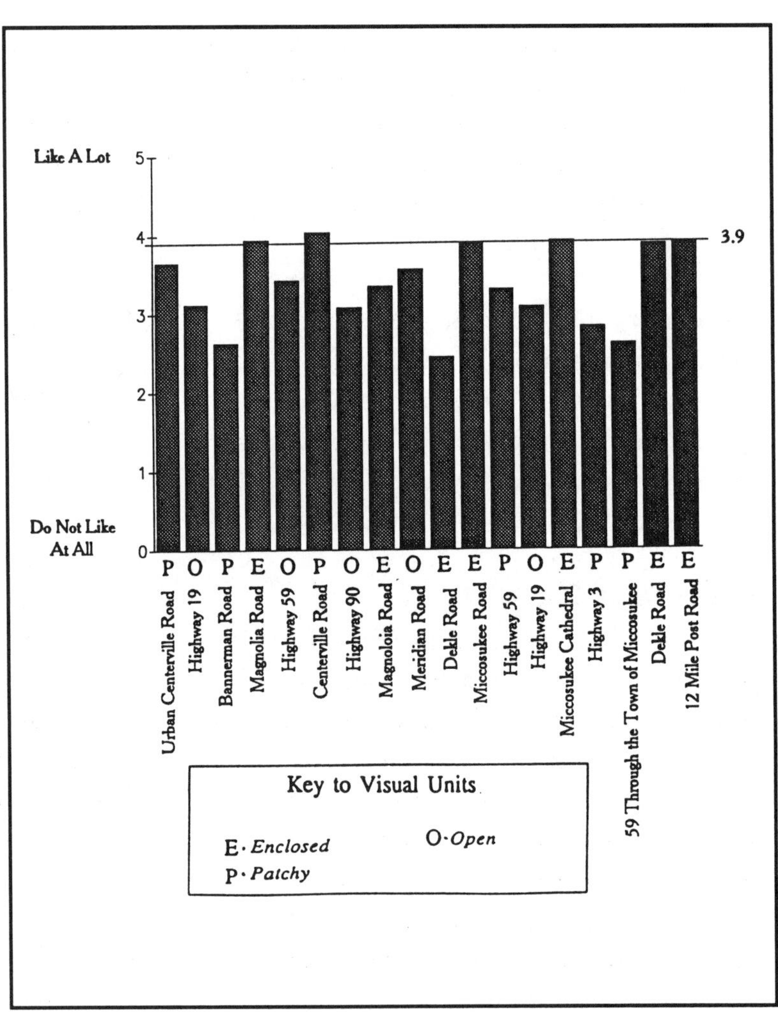

Figure 3.5 *Bar Graphs Depicting Mean Scores for Visual Preference Responses in the Red Hills Case Study.*

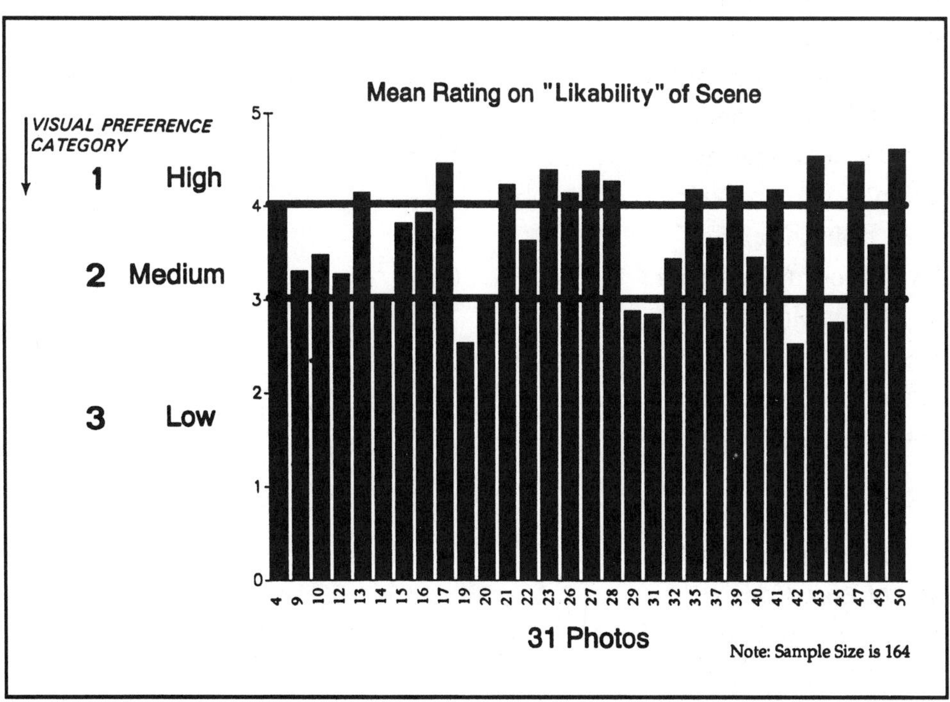

Figure 3.6a *Bar Graph Depicting Mean Scores for Visual Preference Responses in Bluegrass Case Study.*

Landscape type and preference category for the 31 photographs used in the visual preference survey.

Photo #	Landscape Type	Preference Category
4	Horse Farm - modern	1
9	Diversified Agriculture	2
10	Diversified Agriculture	2
12	Horse Farm - modern	2
13	Crossroads Community	1
14	Diversified Agriculture	2
15	Horse Farm - modern	2
16	Diversified Agriculture	2
17	Horse Farm - modern	1
19	Piano Key Development	3
20	Open Road Corridor	2
21	Woodland Savanna	1
22	Diversified Agriculture	2
23	Horse Farm - traditional	1
26	Woodland Savanna	1
27	Horse Farm - traditional	1
28	Horse Farm - traditional	1
29	Open Road Corridor	3
31	Piano Key Development	3
32	Open Road Corridor	2
35	Crossroad Community	1
37	Woodland Savanna	2
39	Horse Farm - modern	1
40	Diversified Agriculture	2
41	Enclosed Road Corridor	1
42	Piano Key Development	3
43	Enclosed Road Corridor	1
45	Crossroad Community	3
47	Enclosed Road Corridor	1
49	Crossroad Community	2
50	Enclosed Road Corridor	1

Figure 3.6b *Landscape Type and Preference Category for Each of the Thirty-one Photographs Listed in Figure 3.6a.*

time, while open road segments and piano key developments were generally ranked the lowest.

One important fact which had to be determined about the 164 respondents who participated in the survey was whether or not they represented the Bluegrass population as a whole. The study team answered this question by collecting demographic data from the respondents and comparing it with 1990 census data from the area under study, including Woodford, Fayette, and Franklin counties. A sample demographic questionnaire was prepared by the study team and attached to the visual preference questionnaire (see Appendix D).

A comparison of the demographic data for the general population of Woodford, Fayette, and Franklin counties with the demographic data on the questionnaire revealed some differences between the respondents and the general population (Fig. 3.7). The differences are slight enough to conclude, however, that the survey respondents adequately represent the people who live in the Inner Bluegrass region.

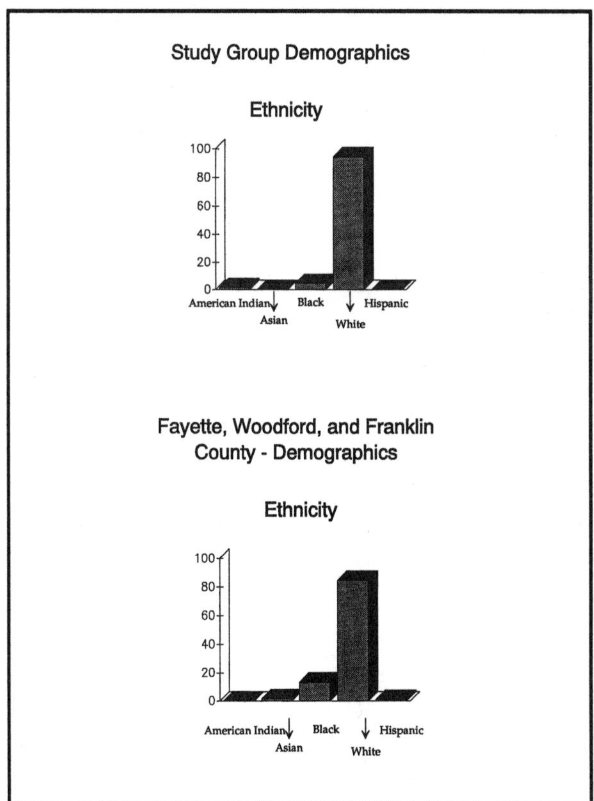

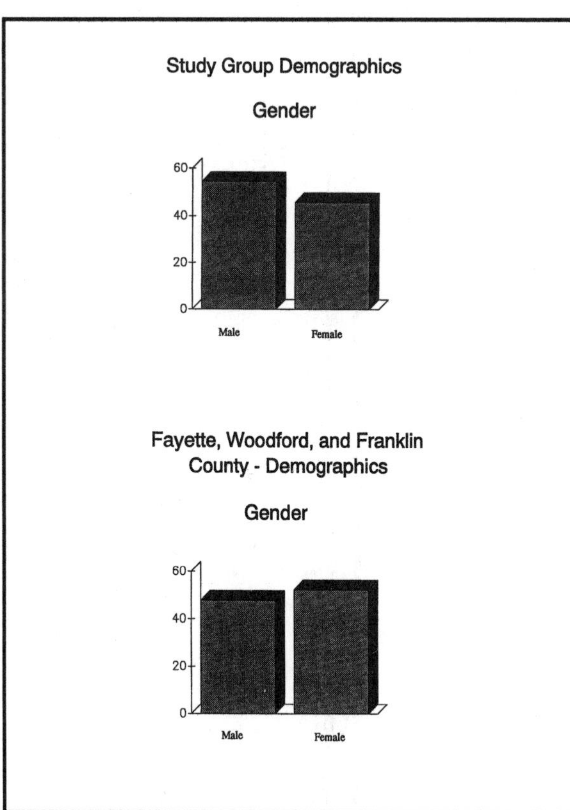

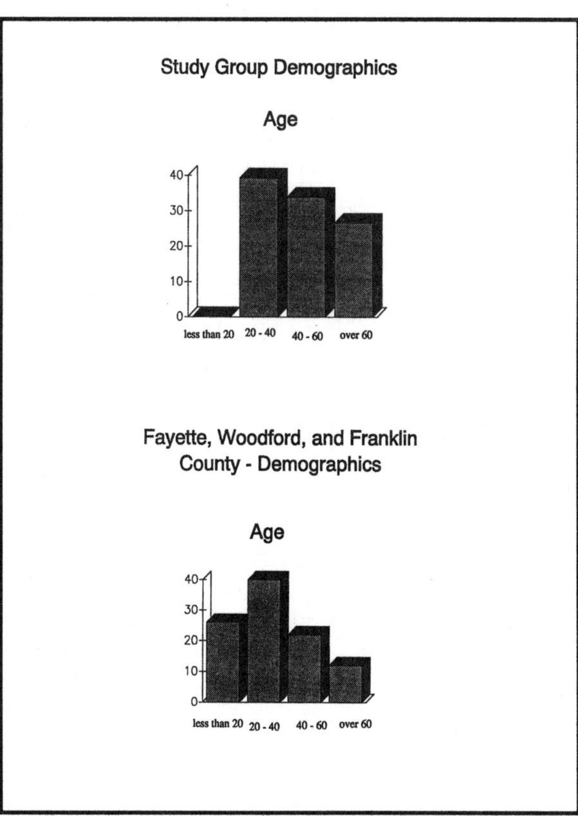

Figure 3.7 *Bar Graphs Comparing Demographic Characteristics of the Respondents with the General Population, Bluegrass Region.*

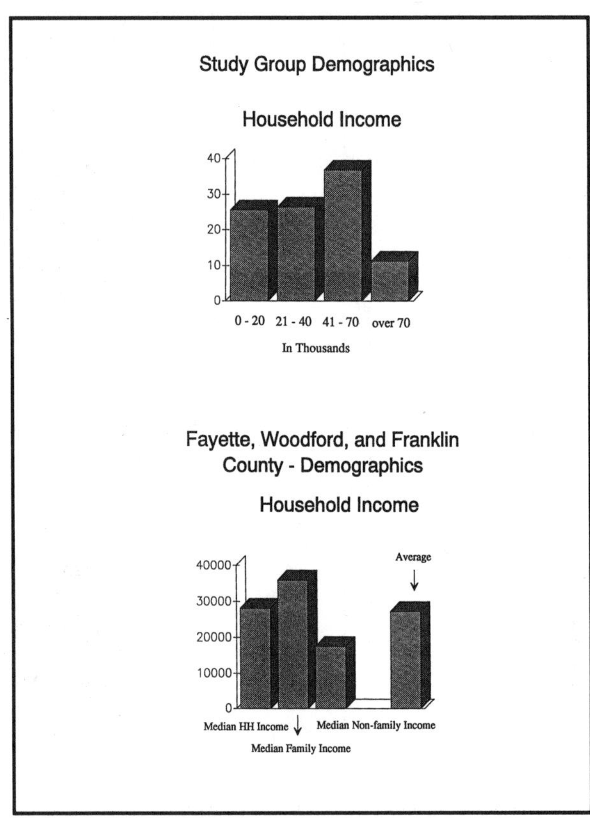

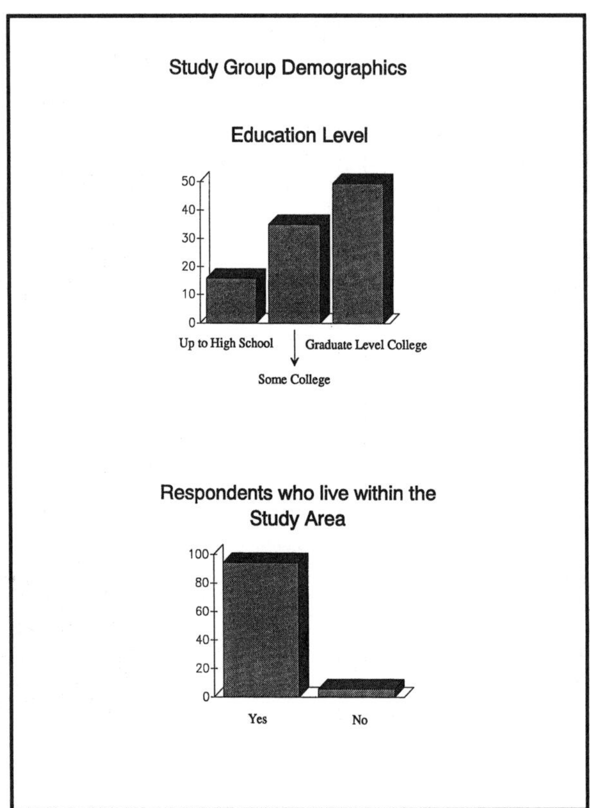

Figure 3.7 (*continued*)

4

Inventory

Before starting the inventory, review the goals of the project. Whatever the emphasis—history, scenery, education, tourism—they must be clearly defined, for they will guide and focus the inventory.

This section describes ways to document and display historic landscape characteristics and visual qualities of road corridors in rural historic landscapes. The inventory serves two main purposes: it records the historic and scenic aspects of road corridors so that protection measures can be developed and effectively implemented; and it serves as a baseline for measuring the progress of implemented protection strategies.

Before starting the inventory, *review the goals of the project*. Whatever the emphasis—history, scenery, education, tourism—they must be clearly defined, for they will guide and focus the inventory. The study team must collect enough data to meet these protection goals and objectives. If the goal is to officially designate a road as historic or scenic, considerably less inventory information may be required than if the goal is to implement a scenic easement program to protect the integrity of road viewsheds.

While compiling data on historic landscape characteristics and scenic patterns, don't ignore other features: roadway surface, right-of-way width, property ownerships, and regulatory boundaries. The inventory may also benefit from a narrative description of the history of each road, that is, reason for its establishment and the places it was meant to connect; reasons why it was important to local commerce and transportation; how it was maintained; and how the road character has changed over time.

Inventories can be conducted by one person, but teamwork is preferable. The team may include local government planning staff, private consultants, volunteers, or any combination of these. Each team member should record particular types of information. For example, one member may record vegetative patterns, while another could log the location and condition of adjacent structures. Photographic documentation might be the responsibility of a third member, while a fourth person could drive. Apart from field work, another team member might be assigned the job of researching the historic significance of the study roads.

Skills needed for conducting the inventory will vary depending on the level of information required. It is essential that someone on the team have the ability to recognize landscape characteristics and visual patterns in the field and log these variables onto recording forms or maps. Topographical map reading skills are also important, since the USGS 7.5-minute quadrangle sheets are commonly used for recording field data. Professions such as environmental planning, forestry, field ecology, geography, landscape architecture, land conservation, and historic preservation all require practitioners to be competent, at some level, in observing, recording, and analyzing field data. People with skills in one or more of these areas should be invited to participate in the inventory.

The inventory process can be divided into a series of steps:

1. Determine type and amount of information needed
2. Compile existing information
3. Construct base maps and recording forms
4. Conduct a windshield or walking survey
5. Organize data

Determine Type and Amount of Information Needed

This is a very important step, for it focuses the inventory and keeps the study team from gathering too much or too little data. As noted earlier, identify the type and amount of information needed based on goals and objectives of the protection program, and the number of roads that will be surveyed.

If the intention is to determine which roads in a regional network are the most historic or scenic, the study team needs to gather enough information to assess historic and scenic significance. Refer back to the Field Guide and Visual Experience chapters to generate a list of historical landscape characteristics and scenic patterns to identify in the field. Also, review the Historical Context section to help guide your research for determining the historical significance and integrity of the roads in the study area.

If the goal is to develop a protection plan for an individual road corridor that has long been valued by the community as very historic or scenic, more detailed information may be necessary. The delineation of the viewshed will define the area of protection, while the identification of property ownerships and regulatory boundaries is essential for understanding how the corridor is currently controlled and managed.

Based on the numbers of roads surveyed and the type and amount of information collected, it is convenient to think of the inventory process in terms of levels. For the purposes of the methodology described in this handbook, a Level I inventory is the survey of a regional system of roads to determine which are the most historic and scenic (Red Hills case study). A Level II inventory is the detailed survey of an individual road corridor so that site-specific protection measures can be developed and implemented within the corridor (Bluegrass case study).

Questions to Ask

How will the inventory be used?

How many roads will be inventoried?

What level of inventory should be conducted?

Based on the goals and objectives of the study, what are the types and amounts of information that should be gathered?

What current corridor conditions need to be described?

What historical information and landscape characteristics will need to be determined?

What types and amount of existing data concerning future land uses and development should be gathered?

Who should conduct the inventory and what special skills are needed?

Compile Existing Information

No matter what the scale of your project, the first documents that should be gathered are maps and aerial photographs. Local libraries or map stores are good sources for topographical maps. The USGS 7.5-minute quadrangles are particularly useful. Road maps and atlases can also be obtained from your local library or map store. District offices of the state department of transportation or county road departments are other sources for good road maps. High-quality aerial photography is often available through state departments of transportation, local planning commissions, and local offices of the Agricultural Stabilization and Conservation Service administered by the United States Department of Agriculture (see Appendix E). County road maps in particular are often very good sources of information about roadway conditions and adjacent structures. Tax maps and aerial photographs are available from the local tax assessor's office. Land use and zoning information is available through local planning commissions.

Any maps that were prepared during the Scenic Advisory Panel meetings (as described in Chapter 3) for displaying visual patterns are an important source of information. Go back and review them and incorporate the data into the inventory if possible.

Potential threats to the integrity of road corridors can be assessed by reviewing local, state, and federal transportation plans to determine if any new roads are planned for the area or if improvements to existing roads are being planned. Road improvement and construction are often the first in a series of changes which threaten the character of rural areas. Local land use and zoning plans should also be reviewed to determine the types of developments which could potentially be constructed in the study area.

There are many resources available which describe the history of a community's roads. First, learn some of the area's history by reviewing secondary sources such as county and state histories, articles in contemporary newspapers, and local college and historical society papers. Talk with long-time residents, who may remember when roads were developed and upgraded or how adjacent scenery has changed over the years.

Primary sources can sometimes reveal actual dates when roads were laid. For instance, many communities created boards or commissions to oversee road construction and maintenance, and their records are often available at the town hall or county courthouse. State archives and road departments may also have information. In particular, state land survey records often include road descriptions as major landmark features.

Other good sources are historic maps and atlases. They can reveal the historic route of a road, its name, and the location of communities, some of which have long since vanished. First-hand accounts of early roads can be found by looking at the journals of explorers, naturalists, military surveyors, settlers, and tourists who sometimes vividly described their travel experience. These accounts are not limited to the roads but also often describe an area's scenery and culture.

Early community boosters often published a range of promotional materials to attract new settlers and development to an area. Railroad atlases, travel guides, newspaper supplements, post cards, and brochures often highlighted a community's road building achievements. Historic photographs from these materials provide clues on how a study area looked in earlier times, and they help to date historic structures, plantings, land uses and division, and important events and activities. Local libraries and state archives collect these materials.

Historic site surveys and National Register nominations for historic properties and historic districts are good sources of information for landmark buildings and historic landscape features that may still remain along a roadway. National Register nominations, available through the state preservation office or The National Register Office in the National Park Service, include photographs, descriptions, statements of significance, sketch maps, topographic maps, and statements for historic context.

Researching the history of a road should reveal how a community developed and utilized the road system for trade, communication, and social interaction. Because building and maintaining roads has always been a front-page issue, a good research source is a community's early newspapers. Although time consuming, this "detective work" is fascinating and a lot of fun.

Questions to Ask

What sources are available to determine the current conditions of road corridors?

What sources are available for determining the historical significance and integrity of road corridors?

What sources are available for data concerning future land use and development pressures?

Construct Base Maps and Recording Forms

Base maps and recording forms are necessary for recording information during the field survey. One of the most straightforward techniques is to log field data directly onto an existing map. USGS 7.5-minute quadrangle sheets are commonly used for field work of all kinds. The scale is 1:24,000 (1 inch equals 2000 feet) but reductions or enlargements can be made depending on the size of the study area. Personnel at local photocopy or blueprinting shops are often very helpful in modifying map scales.

As an inventory aid, consider listing the landscape characteristics identified in Step 1 and prepare a representative symbol for each. The list of characteristics and symbols can be attached to base maps and used as a legend or key (Fig. 4.1). Recording landscape characteristics in the field then becomes a simple matter of applying symbols to the map in the appropriate locations.

Recording forms may also take the form of a matrix. The New York Department of Conservation (NYDEC) has developed a survey matrix for the New York Scenic Roads Program (Fig. 4.2). It consists of a list of landscape characteristics (the "rows") and a series of recording intervals (the "columns"). The recording intervals are determined by the needs and level of detail of the study. The NYDEC matrix uses a recording interval of one mile for the Level I inventory and a one-tenth of a mile interval for the Level II inventory. Landscape characteristics observed within a recording interval are simply checked off in the appropriate box.

Each recording form should contain pertinent information—the date, weather conditions, season of the year, jurisdiction (county or town), name and/or number of

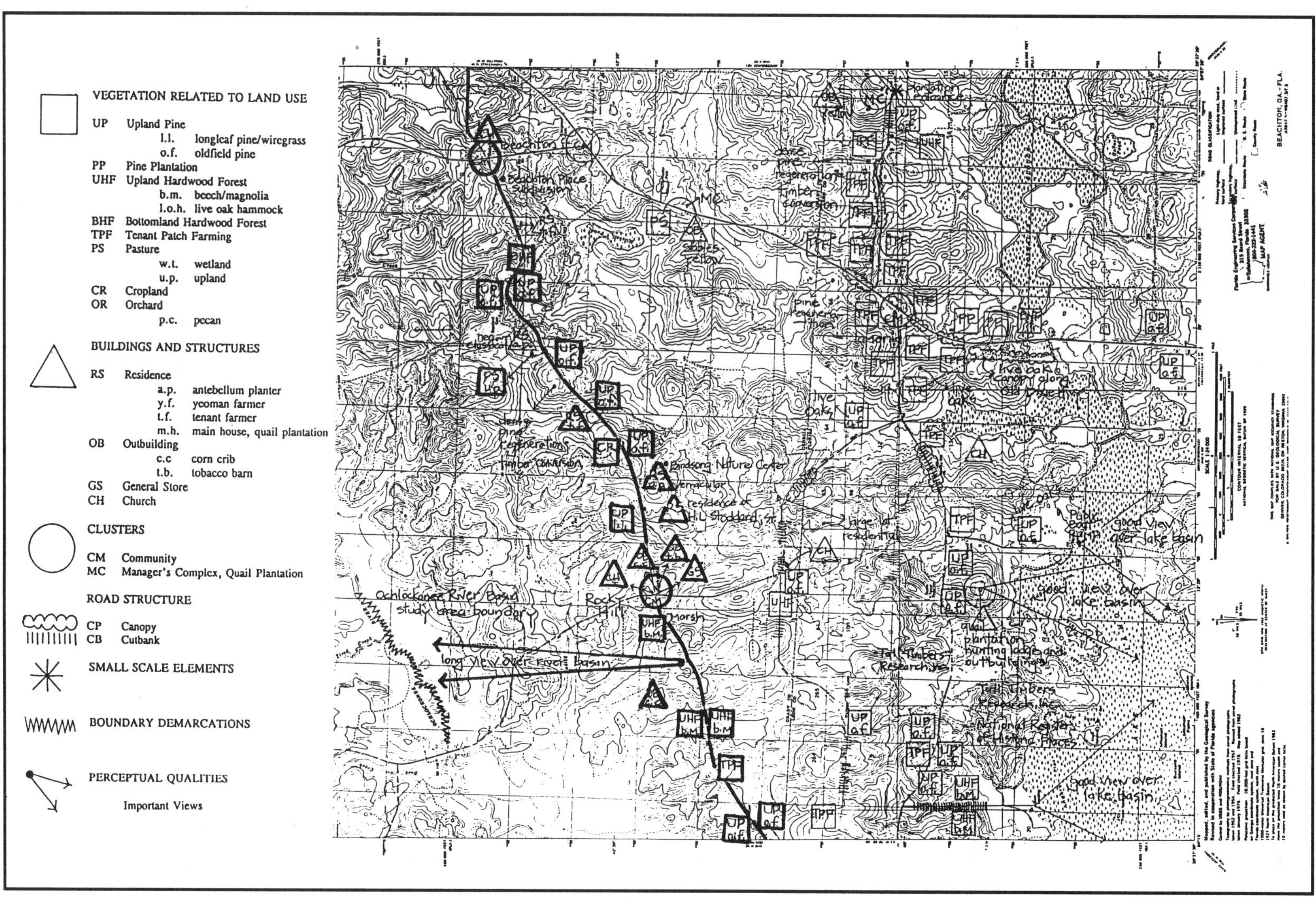

Figure 4.1 *Representative Symbols of Landscape Characteristics. The list of characteristics and symbols can be attached to base maps and used as a legend or key. Recording landscape characteristics in the field then becomes a simple matter of applying symbols to the map in the appropriate locations.*

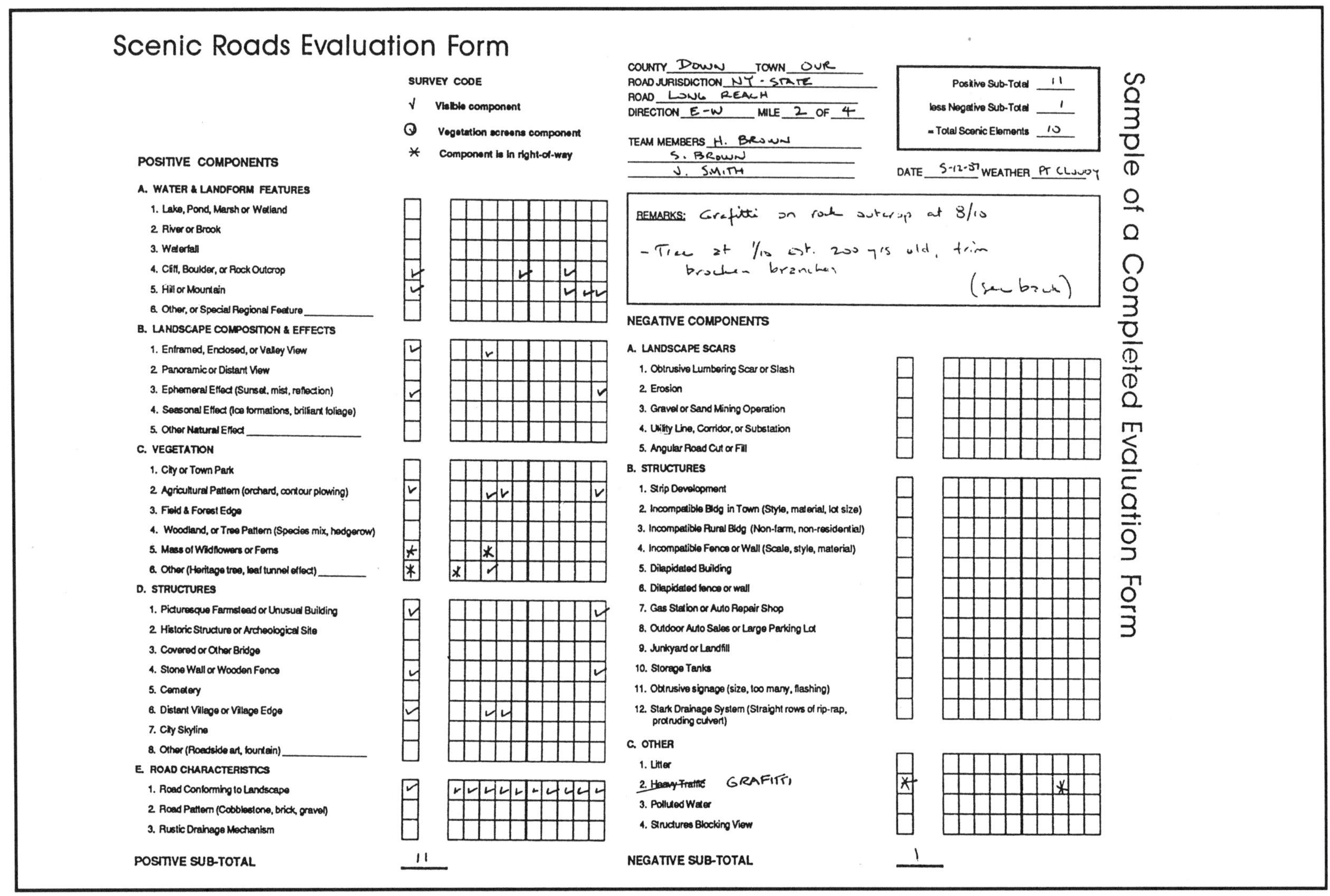

Sample of a Completed Evaluation Form

Scenic Roads Evaluation Form

COUNTY DOWN TOWN OUR
ROAD JURISDICTION NY - STATE
ROAD LONG REACH
DIRECTION E-W MILE 2 OF 4
TEAM MEMBERS H. BROWN
S. BROWN
J. SMITH

Positive Sub-Total 11
less Negative Sub-Total 1
= Total Scenic Elements 10

DATE 5-12-?? WEATHER PT CLOUDY

SURVEY CODE
√ Visible component
Vegetation screens component
✳ Component is in right-of-way

REMARKS: Grafitti on rock outcrop at 8/10
– Tree at ?/10 est. 200 yrs old, trim broken branches
(see back)

POSITIVE COMPONENTS

A. WATER & LANDFORM FEATURES
1. Lake, Pond, Marsh or Wetland
2. River or Brook
3. Waterfall
4. Cliff, Boulder, or Rock Outcrop
5. Hill or Mountain
6. Other, or Special Regional Feature ____

B. LANDSCAPE COMPOSITION & EFFECTS
1. Enframed, Enclosed, or Valley View
2. Panoramic or Distant View
3. Ephemeral Effect (Sunset, mist, reflection)
4. Seasonal Effect (Ice formations, brilliant foliage)
5. Other Natural Effect ____

C. VEGETATION
1. City or Town Park
2. Agricultural Pattern (orchard, contour plowing)
3. Field & Forest Edge
4. Woodland, or Tree Pattern (Species mix, hedgerow)
5. Mass of Wildflowers or Ferns
6. Other (Heritage tree, leaf tunnel effect) ____

D. STRUCTURES
1. Picturesque Farmstead or Unusual Building
2. Historic Structure or Archeological Site
3. Covered or Other Bridge
4. Stone Wall or Wooden Fence
5. Cemetery
6. Distant Village or Village Edge
7. City Skyline
8. Other (Roadside art, fountain) ____

E. ROAD CHARACTERISTICS
1. Road Conforming to Landscape
2. Road Pattern (Cobblestone, brick, gravel)
3. Rustic Drainage Mechanism

POSITIVE SUB-TOTAL 11

NEGATIVE COMPONENTS

A. LANDSCAPE SCARS
1. Obtrusive Lumbering Scar or Slash
2. Erosion
3. Gravel or Sand Mining Operation
4. Utility Line, Corridor, or Substation
5. Angular Road Cut or Fill

B. STRUCTURES
1. Strip Development
2. Incompatible Bldg in Town (Style, material, lot size)
3. Incompatible Rural Bldg (Non-farm, non-residential)
4. Incompatible Fence or Wall (Scale, style, material)
5. Dilapidated Building
6. Dilapidated fence or wall
7. Gas Station or Auto Repair Shop
8. Outdoor Auto Sales or Large Parking Lot
9. Junkyard or Landfill
10. Storage Tanks
11. Obtrusive signage (size, too many, flashing)
12. Stark Drainage System (Straight rows of rip-rap, protruding culvert)

C. OTHER
1. Litter
2. ~~Heavy Traffic~~ GRAFITTI
3. Polluted Water
4. Structures Blocking View

NEGATIVE SUB-TOTAL 1

Figure 4.2 *The NYDEC Survey Matrix. The matrix consists of a list of landscape characteristics (the "rows") and a series of recording intervals (the "columns"). The recording intervals are determined by the needs and level of detail of the study (Shanahan and Smarden).*

road, direction of travel, mile of travel in relationship to total miles (e.g., mile 1 of 4), and name of the survey team members. An area on the recording sheet should also be set aside for comments or remarks.

Questions to Ask

What is the best way to record the current conditions of the road corridors?

What is the best way to record the history of the roads and historical corridor conditions?

What is the best way to record future land uses and development threats?

Conduct a Windshield or Walking Survey

Once existing information has been gathered and the recording forms and/or maps have been prepared, a windshield or walking survey must be conducted so that landscape characteristics can be documented. For each road, the survey team starts from a fixed landmark and slowly moves down the roadway, identifying landscape characteristics.

If the survey team is recording data on a map, symbols representing the landscape characteristics can be logged onto the map at the appropriate location. If using a matrix, stop the car at the end of each recording interval and simply check the appropriate boxes to indicate the presence of particular characteristics. Recording data in one direction at a time is helpful, for it may prevent missing hard-to-see characteristics.

Photographs can serve to quickly and easily communicate existing conditions and document baseline information to measure future changes. Select photographic viewpoints along the road which best represent visually distinct areas. Viewpoints should be indicated on your map or recording form, and photos taken from that viewpoint should be matched with the same number (Fig. 4.3).

Questions to Ask

How should the survey team be organized?

What mode of transportation should be used for the survey?

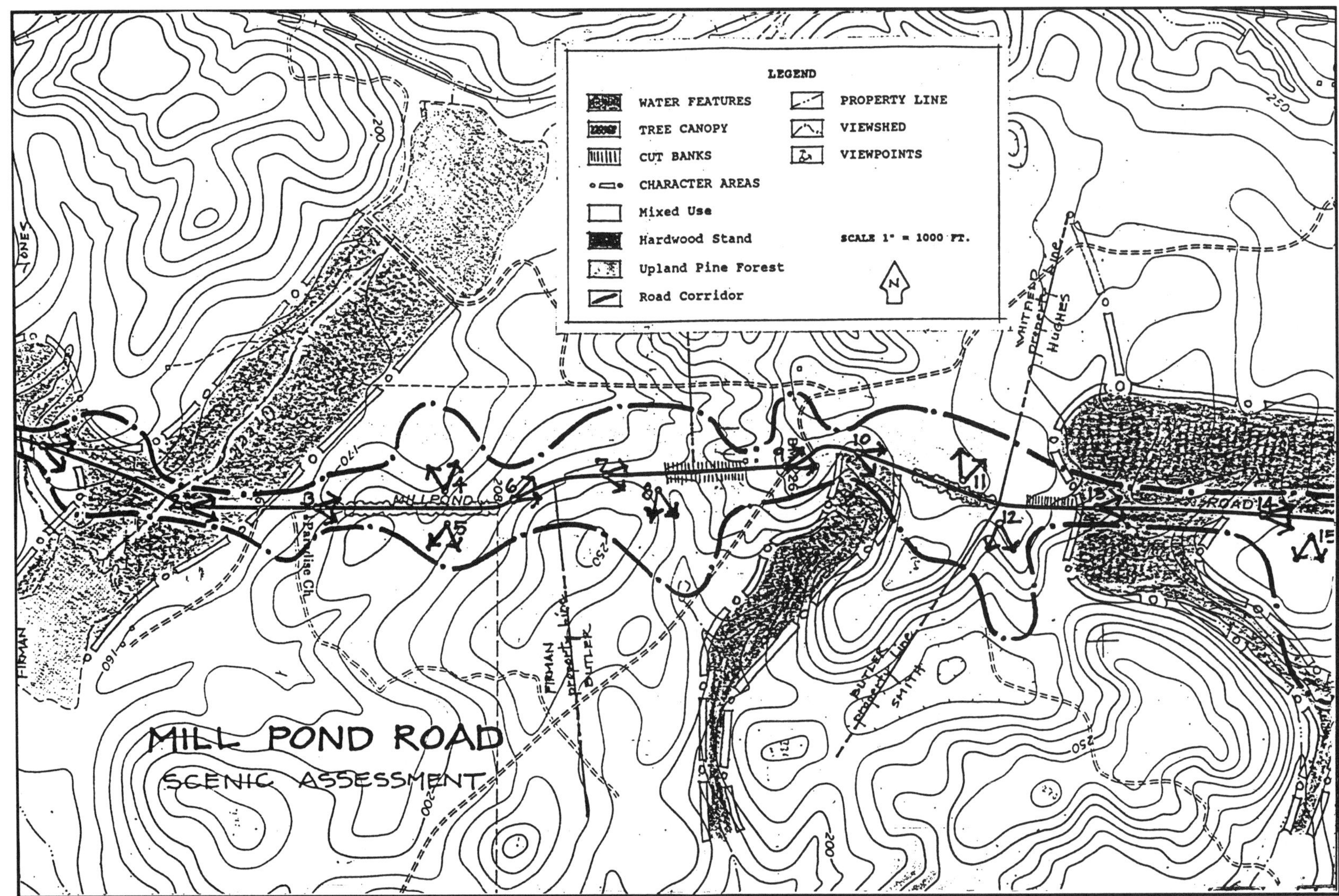

Figure 4.3 *Selected Viewpoints that Best Represent Visually Distinct Areas.*

Should the conditions of the road corridor be documented by photographs?

If so, how shall viewpoints be selected?

How much time should be budgeted for the field survey?

Organize Data

Organization of information collected thus far will facilitate the orderly application of evaluation criteria presented in the next chapter. The way the data is organized will depend on the type of study. For a Level I inventory, assemble inventory sheets by road name and identify road segments by mile marker or other clear unit of measurement.

For the Level II inventory, organization of the data into *management units* is helpful. Management units are areas within the corridor that have similar combinations of roadside conditions, landscape characteristics, and visual patterns (refer to Fig. 4.9 in the Bluegrass case study).

For the information collected in the inventory process to be used for decision-making, it must be easily accessible. A simple, effective filing system is best. Label roads as simply as possible, either numerically or by road name. Photocopy the original forms and photos, and file copies separately.

If maps have been used to record information, it may be useful to photocopy segments of the road corridor onto smaller sheets, such as standard letter size (Fig. 4.4), and arrange the photocopies in a 3-ring binder. The original maps may then be stored in a map file. Check with a local office supply business to determine the best map filing system for the needs of the project.

Questions to Ask

How should roads or road segments be organized to best facilitate an evaluation?

What is the best way to file recording forms? What is the best way to file maps?

What is the best way to file accompanying photographs?

MILL POND ROAD

History/Historic Sites

Located two miles south of Thomasville, Mill Pond Road was earlier known as Linton Mill Road. In the nineteenth century, John Lanier Linton and his son-in-law Thomas Clark Wyche operated a saw mill, grist mill and cotton gin at the thirty acre scenic pond. By his death in 1870, Wyche had amassed about 1600 acres, and left his estate to his daughter, Alice, who had married Linton. They purchased adjoining lots and by 1885 Mill Pond Plantation consisted of over 3,000 acres.[19]

In 1903, Jeptha H. Wade, a wealthy Cleveland financier and philanthropist, purchased Mill Pond. He increased his Thomas County landholdings to over 10,000 acres and in 1905 built a unique Mediterranean style mansion designed by the Cleveland architectural firm of Hubbell and Benes. Wade hired Warren H. Manning of Boston, the designer of the Biltmore gardens in Asheville, to lay out the Mill Pond landscaping.[20] Part of Manning's design included the construction of two overpasses on Mill Pond Road. Spanning 32 feet, these wood plank and steel girder bridges still enable hunting wagons to pass over Mill Pond Road.

To a large degree, the 7.2 mile Mill Pond Road could be considered a private plantation road, as both sides of the road are surrounded by hunting estates. Old abandoned tenant dwellings are scattered along the road, reflecting the dominant role black farmers played on these estates.

While this historic road meanders through Mill Pond Plantation, the sprawling main house is out of sight as it overlooks the spillway. Although the traveller now can only hear the sounds of the waterfall, it is not hard to imagine the grinding of the millstone that once was here.

Visual Quality

Like New Hope Road, Mill Pond Road conveys the scenic experience of a private drive through the middle of these great hunting plantations. The 22 foot wide dirt road is bordered by park-like pine forest and small patch fields. Other segments contain columns of stately live oaks forming a green canopy. In a low-lying area, cypress swamps bring a mystical quality to the road. Other than the graffiti "Paige loves Alan" on the trestle of the old bridge, human encroachment has not marred this historic roadway.

At the end of the seven mile journey through this green forest, the monumental Birdwood Mansion seems to welcome visitors back to civilization. This Neo-Classical house, built in 1930, now serves as the administration building for Thomas Community College. Shortly beyond is the city of Thomasville.

182

LEGEND

VEGETATION
Upland Pine
Pine Plantation
Upland Hardwood Forest
Bottomland Hardwoods
Orchard

Pasture
Cropland
Tenant Patch Farming

BUILDING / STRUCTURE
Residence
Outbuilding
General Store
Church
School

CLUSTERS
Community
Manager's Complex

SMALL SCALE ELEMENTS

PERCEPTUAL QUALITIES

ORIENTATION

Road: Mill Pond
Quad Sheet: Thomasville
Scale 1 : 24,000
North

CC
Matchline

DESCRIPTION
residential subdivision
hardwood, screen
filtered view of Mill Pond
Mill Pond dam
hardwoods in drainage
upland hardwood, screen
private bridge, Warren Manning designed
upland pine
tenant patch farming
bottomland hardwood
private bridge, Warren Manning designed
filtered view of longleaf in drainage
"viewshed - watershed"
upland pine, longleaf
tenant cabin
Fletcher Rd., private
upland pine, longleaf
cutbanks
upland hardwoods, drainage
Matchline
BB

185

Figure 4.4 *Road Segment Photocopied onto an 8.5 x 11 Inch Sheet from a Larger Inventory Map. Using this format, the inventory can easily be stored in a 3-ring binder along with narrative descriptions.*

Red Hills Case Study

Landscape characteristics for this Level I inventory were first delineated on USGS 7.5-minute topographical maps during a windshield survey. This information was later traced onto 8.5 x 11 inch mylar (vinyl) sheets. The mylar sheets are easily revised, which makes it simple to record changes in the landscape as they occur over time. Also, mylar sheets can be rapidly photocopied and taped together to provide a quick and complete map of the whole road corridor or particular segments (Fig. 4.4).

Bluegrass Case Study

The Bluegrass case study was a Level II inventory that documented the major landscape characteristics and visual qualities of the Old Frankfort Pike and Pisgah Pike road corridors. Site specific roadside conditions, landscape features, and visual patterns were documented along the two study roads. Based on an analysis of the inventory, management units were delineated so that strategies and techniques aimed at protecting and enhancing the scenic character of the road corridors could be effectively developed and applied.

The study team spent two days on the roads (26 miles total) conducting a windshield survey by which existing conditions were recorded onto base maps consisting of modified USGS 7.5-minute quadrangle sheets. Modifications included the enlargement of the map scale from 1:24,000 (1 inch = 2000 feet) to 1:12,000 (1 inch = 1000 feet) and the exaggeration of the roadway width so that roadside conditions could be described without obscuring important physiographical information (Fig. 4.5).

Landscape components (Fig. 4.6) were located and categorized in terms of *adjacent land use* (corresponding to landscape types as described in Chapter 2); *eye level features* (fencing, vegetation, and embankments); and *overhead features* (tree canopy and utility transmission lines). These categories are a logical grouping of the major components most affecting the visual character of the road corridors. The relationship of the three categories (or management layers) served as the basis

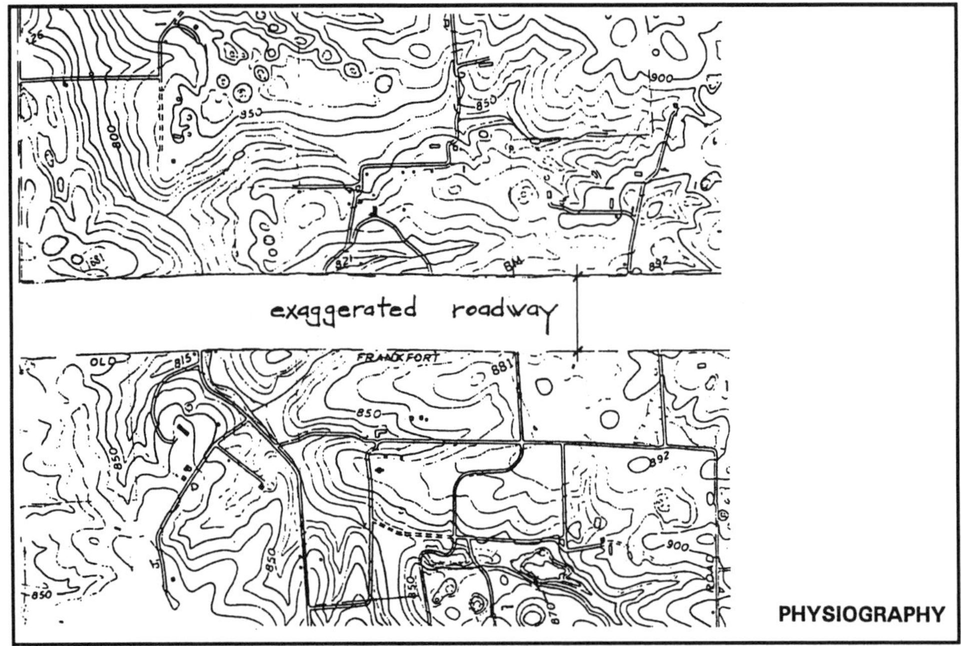

Figure 4.5

Physiography. The roadway width was exaggerated so that roadside conditions could be documented without obscuring important physiological information.

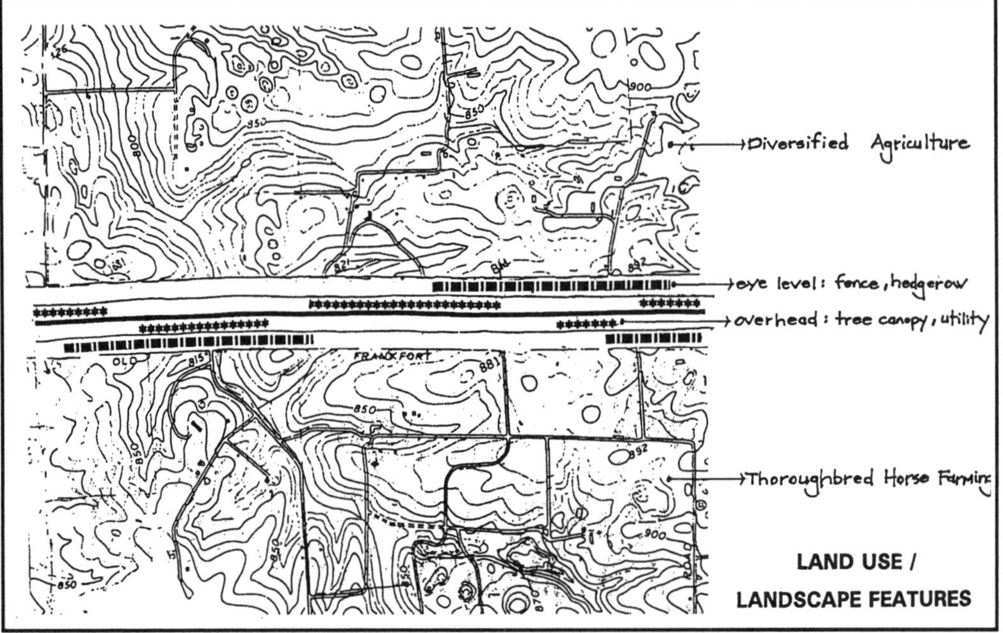

Figure 4.6

Land Use/Landscape Features. Adjacent land use, eye level features, and overhead features are groupings of major components which most affect the visual character of a road corridor.

for the development of the management units discussed later in this chapter.

A visual analysis (Fig. 4.7) was conducted which included the delineation of the viewshed and view types. The *viewshed* is the area of landscape that can be seen from any given point along the roads. Mapping the visible landscape along the length of a route is essential for defining the width of corridor for which protection strategies and techniques will be applied. *View types*, classified as open, filtered, or enclosed, are influenced predominately by the eye level features such as fencing, vegetation, and embankments. View types influence the perception of the landscape and provide clues for managing roadside features to preserve and enhance scenic qualities.

Property ownerships (Fig. 4.8) were delineated using Woodford and Fayette County tax parcel maps. Owner's names were not identified at this stage, although that information will be required when landowner contacts must be made.

Except for the relatively small strip of publicly owned right-of-way, most of the land in the road corridors is privately owned. Because corridor protection will rely heavily on adjacent landowners, the management team will need to work closely with them to effectively implement long-term protection strategies and techniques. Knowledge of boundary lines and key landowners is essential to this step.

Based on the analysis of the inventory of roadside conditions, landscape characteristics, and visual patterns, management units were devised. The units allow for an orderly application of protection strategies and techniques. Thirteen management unit types were defined within the two corridors, ranging in length from several hundred feet to several miles (Fig. 4.9).

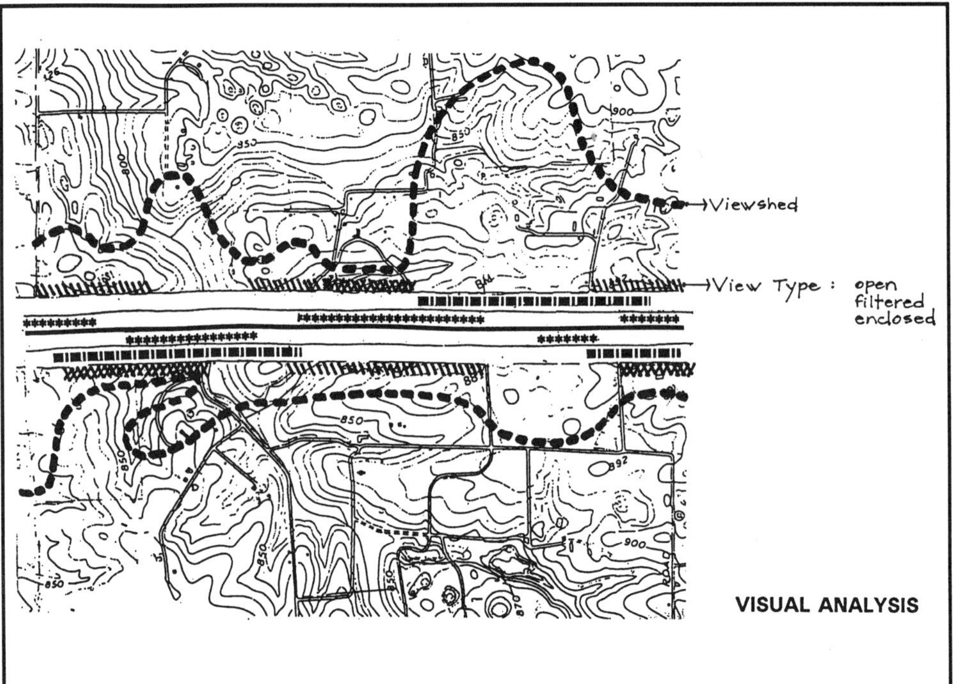

Figure 4.7

Visual Analysis. The documentation of viewsheds and view types provides a basis for managing the perceptual qualities of a road corridor.

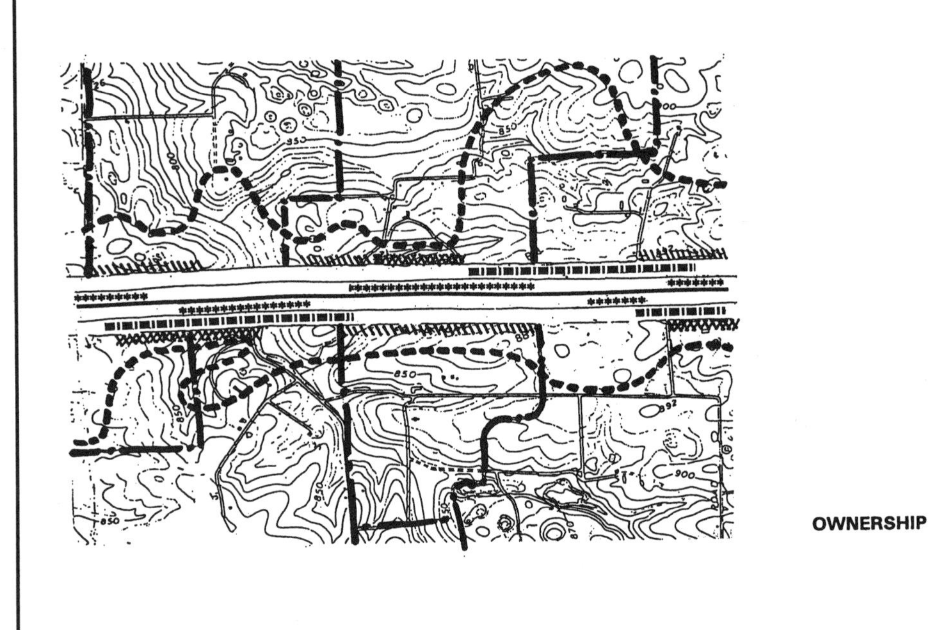

Figure 4.8

Land Ownership. Establishing the pattern of ownership is essential for determining how the corridor is currently controlled and managed.

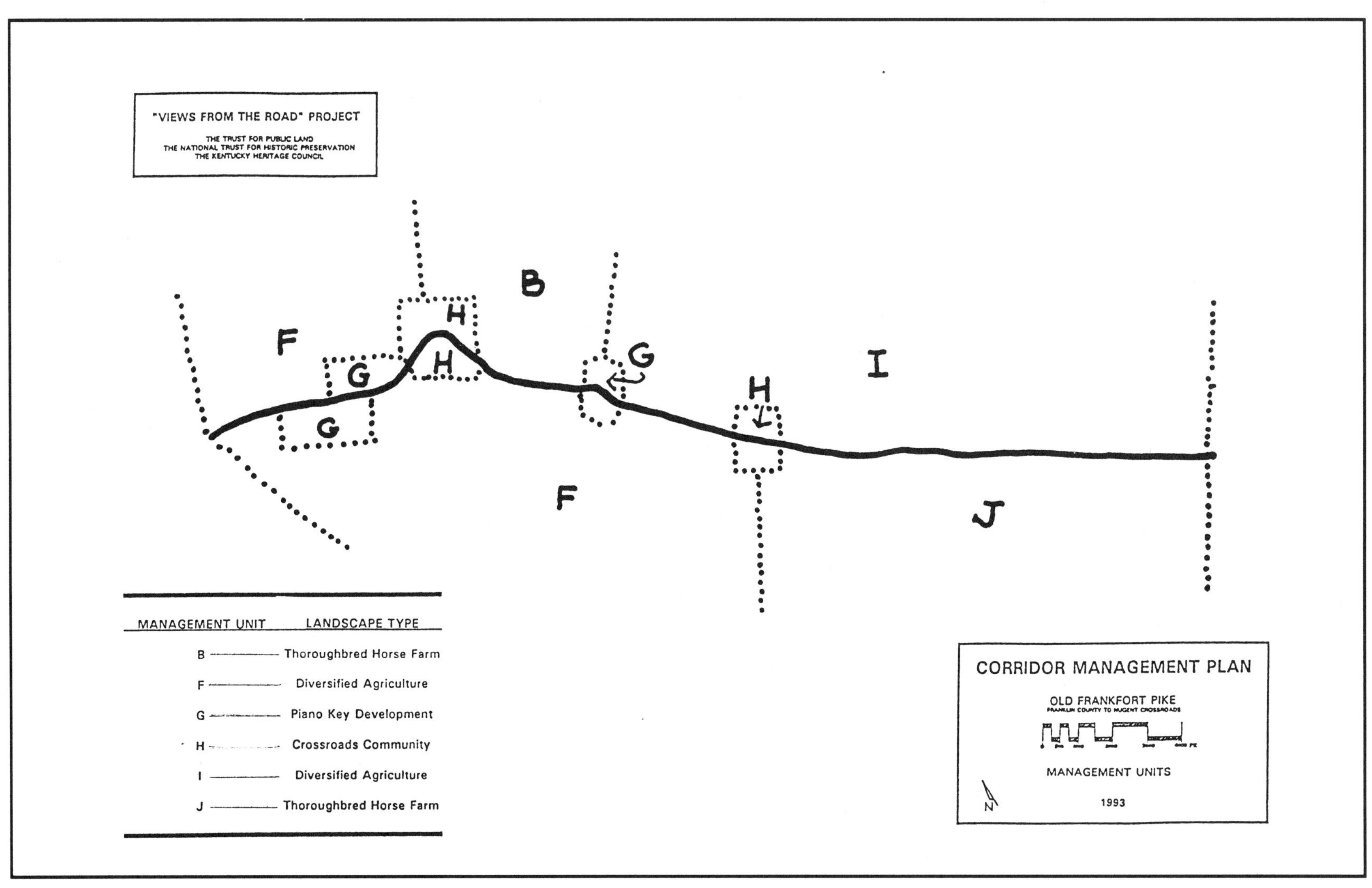

Figure 4.9 *Management Units as Applied to a Segment of the Old Frankfort Pike, Bluegrass Case Study.*

5

EVALUATION

Evaluation criteria are a set of standards for judging the importance of road corridors or segments, relative to one another. Criteria should be developed based on project goals.

This chapter explores ways to evaluate the overall significance of roads or road segments within a regional network. Factors for the study team to consider in selecting and ranking these evaluation criteria are presented and a method for classifying roads is described.

As with all steps in this handbook's methodology, the study team should be the primary decision makers when evaluating the road corridors. While assistance from professionals should certainly not be overlooked, the knowledge and community input gained from the previous steps will provide more than enough background to enable team members to arrive at solid conclusions about the significance of each corridor.

Selection of Evaluation Criteria

Evaluation criteria are a set of standards for judging the importance of road corridors or segments, relative to one another. Criteria should be developed based on project goals. For example, criteria for protecting historic and scenic roadways would include historic significance, historic integrity, and scenic value. Other considerations may include: tourism benefits, recreational value, educational/ interpretive value, vulnerability and threats to scenic and historic integrity from land development, and political considerations, including community interest for protecting particular roads.

Listed below are some of the more commonly used evaluation criteria. Use the list as a guide and modify it to suit the needs of your program.

Historic Value

This criteria is used to determine the historic value of a road in terms of its conveyance of a sense of "place," historic significance and integrity, and presence of remaining adjacent historic components.

Conveyance of a Sense of Place

Does the road strongly convey to the traveler a distinctive historical sense of place through its visual and aesthetic relationship between landscape, buildings, and structures which unify and define the area?

Significance and Integrity of the Road

Is the road significant to the area's history, and does it retain significant historic features, such as historic route, vegetation patterns, paving system, or other features?

Presence of Remaining Adjacent Historic Resources

Do adjacent historic resources contribute significantly to the historic character of the roadway?

Scenic Value

Evaluate a road's scenic value in terms of roadway condition, scenic views, visually preferred travel experiences, and compatibility of adjacent cultural features.

Roadway Condition

Does the roadway conform to the landscape in a pleasing way? Does the immediate roadway provide a pleasing driving experience?

Scenic Viewsheds

Does the road corridor contain scenic or pastoral views, such as cropland and pastures, water bodies, and forests, that reflect undisturbed open space, green belts, and viewsheds which greatly enhance the overall visual quality of the area?

Visual Preference

Does the roadway possess those visual qualities which are most preferred by the residents of the area as determined by a visual preference survey of the local population?

Land Development

Is the roadway relatively free from intrusive development, powerlines, or other features which would adversely impact the scenic quality of the roadway?

Interpretive or Educational Value

This criteria assesses the educational value of a road by determining the presence and variety of adjacent historic resources, the historic periods represented by these resources, and the relationship of the road to the historic network.

Presence and Variety of Remaining Adjacent Historic Resources

Do adjacent historic resources contribute significantly to the visual variety and character of the roadway? Are there a variety of landscape characteristics visible from the road?

Representation of Historic Periods

Do the visible landscape characteristics represent the full range of historic periods?

Relationship to the Historic Road Network

Does the road provide an important link in the historic circulation network?

Threats/Vulnerability

This is a criteria to determine threats of cultural modifications and levels of existing protection (if any).

Threats of Cultural Modifications

Is the roadway threatened by intrusive development, powerlines, or other features which would adversely impact the scenic quality and historic integrity of the roadway?

Level of Protection

Is the road officially designated as historic or scenic by a local, state, or federal agency? Is the road corridor currently protected by regulatory measures such as land use regulations and zoning ordinances or nonregulatory measures such as conservation easements?

Political Considerations

This criteria is applied to determine the effects that multiple governmental jurisdictions may have on the road, the likelihood of their cooperation in administering a protection program, and the degree of community interest and support for protecting particular roads.

Likelihood of Inter-Governmental Cooperation

How many governmental jurisdictions does the road traverse? What is the likelihood of inter-governmental cooperation in implementing a protection program?

Community Support

Is there a high degree of community interest in protecting a particular road?

Questions to Ask

Based on the goals and objectives of the study, what evaluation criteria should be selected?

Ranking the Criteria

In order to apply the criteria, the study group must define a set of conditions or requirements for each criterion so that a value can be assigned to each road or road segment. For the sake of simplicity, it's usually best to use relatively few value categories. Three categories—high, medium, and low, or 1, 2, and 3—should suffice (Fig. 5.1).

Because communities value the criteria differently, weighting systems which reflect the relative importance of the criteria may be necessary. For example, the study team may determine from its work with community members that roads or road segments which provide a historic travel experience should receive preservation priority. These roads may not be especially scenic, so the value assigned to the historic integrity criterion must be sufficiently weighted to reflect its relative importance (Fig. 5.2).

Questions to Ask

What set of requirements should be established for each criterion? Should professional assistance be obtained for ranking selected critertia?

How many value categories should be assigned?

Should the criteria be weighted to reflect the greater importance of some over others?

Application of Criteria: Assigning Values

After the study team ranks the evaluation criteria (weighted if necessary), they must review the inventory and assign a value to each road which reflects the criteria rankings. If there is not enough information to assign a value for a particular criterion, insufficient information was gathered during the inventory stage. Collect more data so that a value can be assigned.

CRITERIA	VALUE
Historic	
high significance/integrity	3
medium significance/integrity	2
low significance/integrity	1
Scenic	
high visual preference	3
medium visual preference	2
low visual preference	1

Figure 5.1
Ranking the Criteria (hypothetical model).

CRITERIA	VALUE	WEIGHTING FACTOR	WEIGHTED VALUE
Historic			
high significance/integrity	3	X2	6
medium significance/integrity	2	X2	4
low significance/integrity	1	X2	2
Scenic			
high visual preference	3	X1	3
medium visual preference	2	X1	2
low visual preference	1	X1	1

Figure 5.2
Weighting the Criteria (hypothetical model).

CRITERIA ↓	ROADS → MILL POND	SPRINGHILL
Historic	3	1
Scenic	1	3
Total Score	4	4

CRITERIA	VALUE
Historic	
high significance/integrity	3
medium significance/integrity	2
low significance/integrity	1
Scenic	
high visual preference	3
medium visual preference	2
low visual preference	1

CRITERIA ↓	ROADS → MILL POND	SPRINGHILL
Historic	6	2
Scenic	1	3
Total Score	7	5

CRITERIA	VALUE	WEIGHTING FACTOR	WEIGHTED VALUE
Historic			
high significance/integrity	3	X2	6
medium significance/integrity	2	X2	4
low significance/integrity	1	X2	2
Scenic			
high visual preference	3	X1	3
medium visual preference	2	X1	2
low visual preference	1	X1	1

Figure 5.3 *Application of Unweighted and Weighted Criteria (hypothetical matrix). Note that when historic criteria is weighted, Mill Pond Road ranks higher than Springhill Road.*

The evaluation matrix is a well-established planning tool for applying criteria to determine the overall importance of a resource. A matrix is nothing more than a thorough checklist for tallying criteria scores in a way that allows for easy comparison (Fig. 5.3).

Questions to Ask

Did the inventory provide enough information to assign a value to each road for each criterion? If not, what data is lacking?

Is the evaluation matrix the best tool for applying criteria and displaying the results? If so, how should the matrix be constructed to suit the needs of the study?

Road/Landscape Classification

Assign an overall value to each road based on the tabulation of values (or scores) for each criterion. Use the composite score to classify the roads or road segments, from highest to lowest. This classification will help to guide the development of protection strategies for the roads, either in a regional network or for the management units within a single road corridor (see case studies for examples).

Questions to Ask

How should the classification be interpreted for the development of protection measures for the roads?

Red Hills Case Study

The major goals of the Red Hills landscape assessment are to enhance public awareness of and appreciation for the special landscape resources of the Red Hills and to preserve the historic integrity and scenic qualities of the region's rural roads. Criteria were developed which reflected historic, scenic, and interpretive value.

Each criterion was ranked by establishing a set of conditions so that a high, medium, or low value could be assigned to each road in terms of how well it satisfied those conditions (refer to Fig. 5.4).

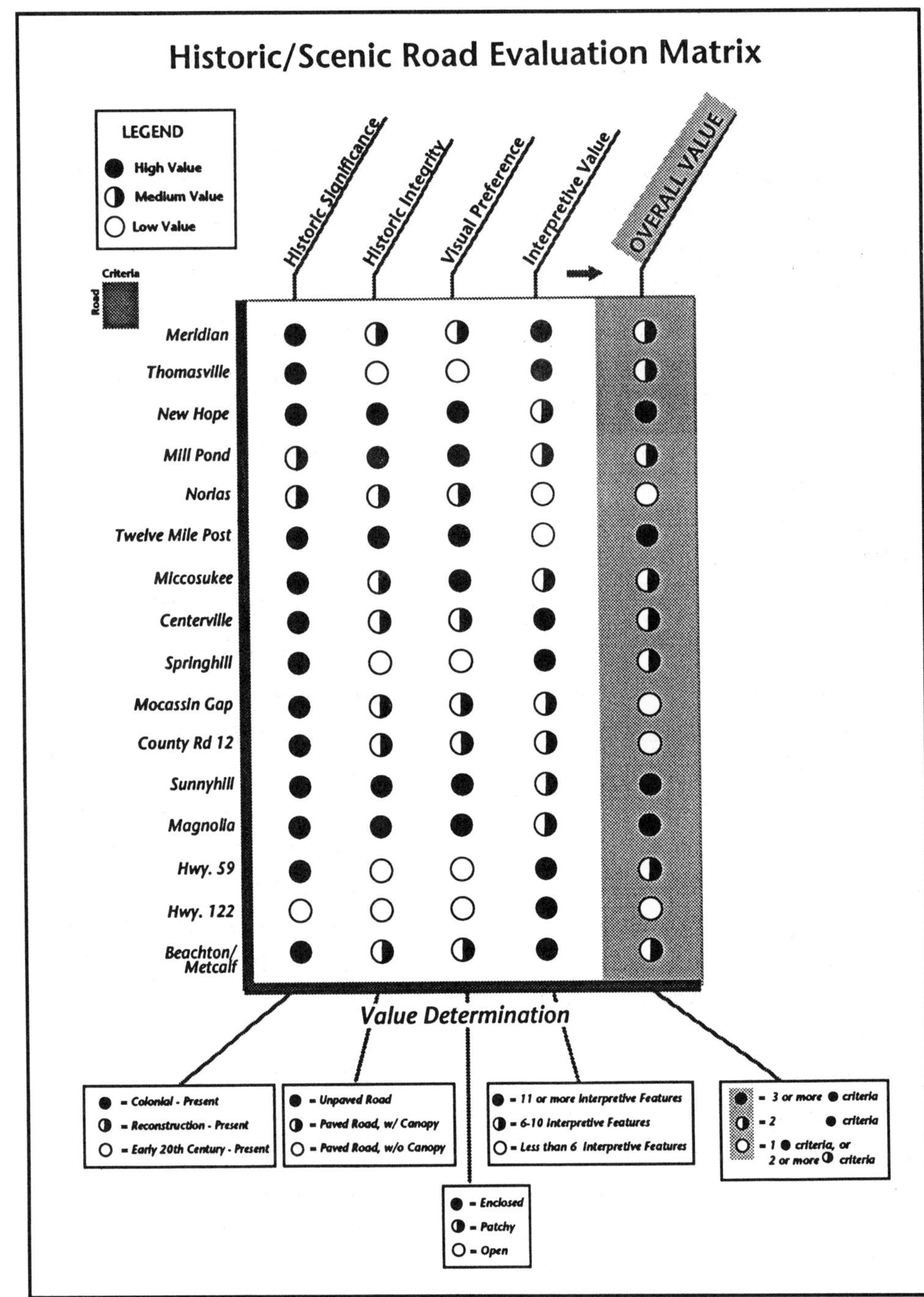

Figure 5.4
Red Hills Matrix.

The evaluation criteria were applied to each road in the study area through the use of a standard evaluation matrix. After reviewing the inventory, each road was assigned a value for each of the four criteria: historical significance, historical integrity, visual preference, and interpretation.

To determine the relative overall value of each road, the values for all criteria were added together and averaged. Roads with the highest overall value were designated as Class "A," medium-ranked roads were Class "B," and Class "C" roads were those that ranked lowest.

The evaluation matrix and map of road classes served as tools for determining appropriate levels of protection for the different categories of roads. The location and relationship of roads and road classes is provided in Figure 5.5.

Bluegrass Case Study

The Bluegrass case study involved the evaluation of the management units determined from the Level II inventory. The aim of the evaluation was to determine the visual preference level of the management units described in Chapter 4.

Generally, the most preferred landscape types in the Bluegrass study area are the thoroughbred horse farm, enclosed road segment, and woodland savanna. Diversified agriculture and crossroads communities received medium scores most of the time, while open road segments and piano key developments were generally ranked the lowest.

The major landscape type of each management unit was compared with the corresponding landscape type in the visual preference survey results. A high, medium, or low value was assigned to each management unit based on this comparison (Fig. 5.6).

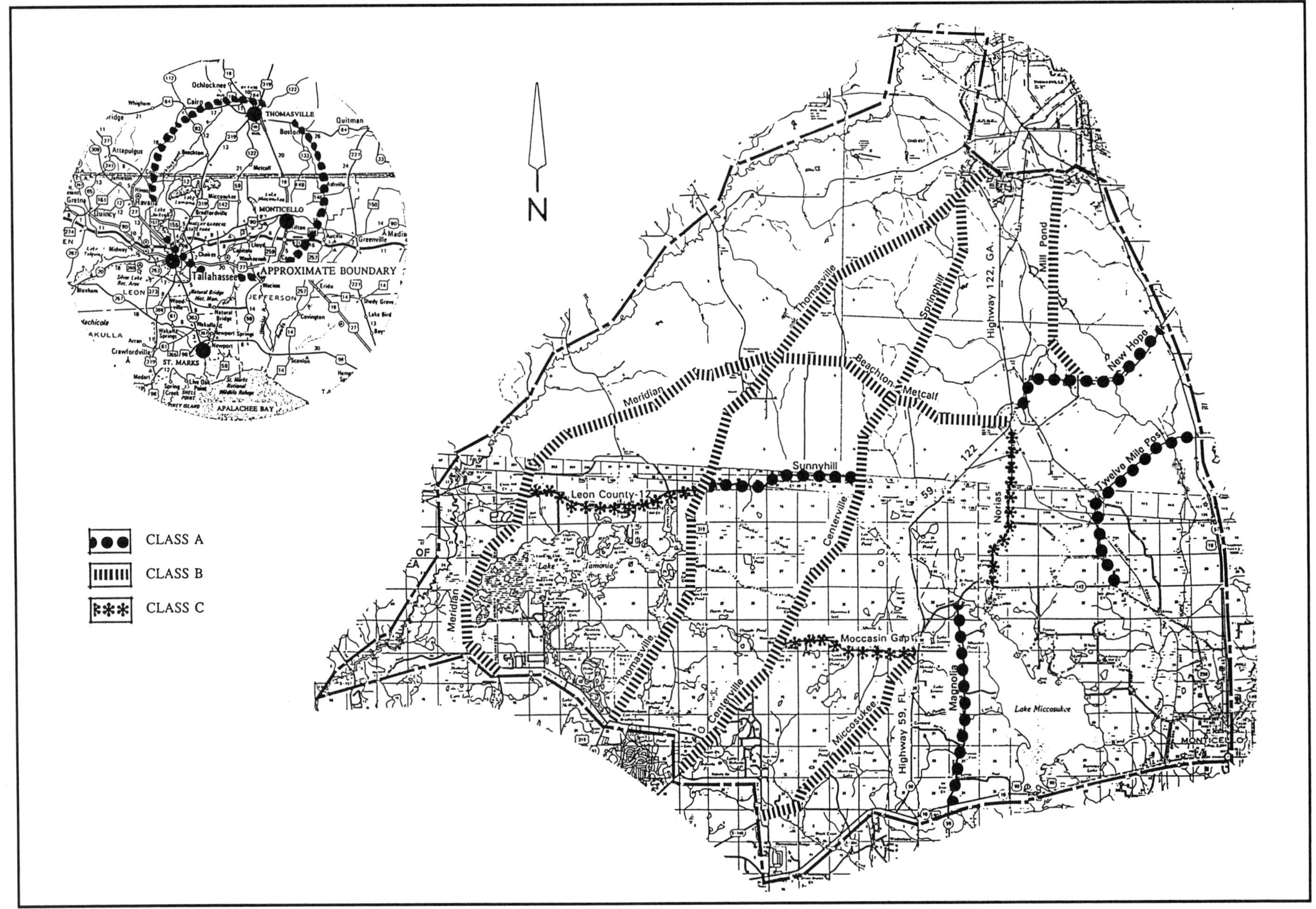

Figure 5.5 *Red Hills Road Classes.*

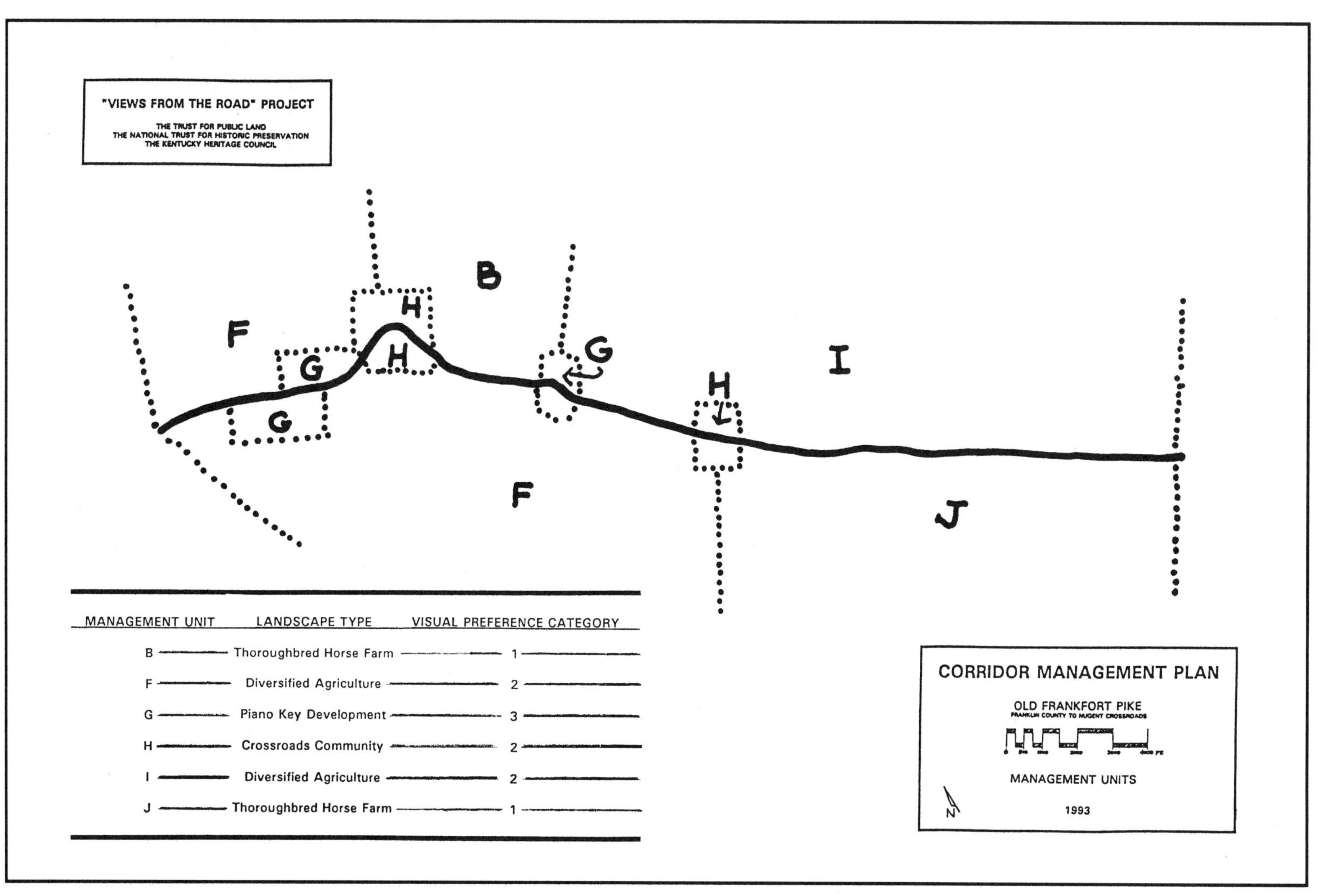

Figure 5.6 *Application of Visual Preference Categories to Management Units along a Segment of Old Frankfort Pike, Bluegrass Case Study.*

6

Protection Strategies and Techniques

Corridor management planning is most effective when government agencies, business organizations, conservation organizations, community groups, and landowners work in partnership to implement a range of creative techniques and solutions.

This chapter discusses strategies and techniques to accomplish the ultimate goal of this handbook's assessment process: historic and scenic road protection. Several nonregulatory and regulatory measures are presented, along with a discussion of their effectiveness. Success stories from other communities around the country are also highlighted.

Exploring Protection Options

Protection techniques fall into two broad categories: *nonregulatory measures* (from both landowners and public agencies) and *regulatory measures*. Included under nonregulatory measures are low cost, community-initiated strategies for community groups, local land trusts, and others identified as "voluntary techniques." The options are organized by effectiveness, from those that provide the least amount of protection to those that offer the greatest degree of protection for roads and the adjacent landscape. (See Table 6.1 for a quick reference guide.)

It is important to make the distinction between *direct* and *indirect* protection. While educational initiatives do not provide the direct protection of regulatory measures, they are essential for building the broad base of community support for adopting restrictive measures such as land use and zoning controls. In this sense, community education provides effective *indirect* protection.

The definitions provided below for each strategy are intended only to give handbook users a general explanation. For more information, refer to the two primary references from which the definitions were taken: Stokes, *Saving America's Countryside;* and Mantell, *Creating Successful Communities* (see citations in the bibliography).

Nonregulatory (Voluntary) Techniques

Educational Initiatives

Educational initiatives include techniques which increase public awareness of historic and scenic road corridors and the need to protect them. Through education, controversial regulatory measures such as land use and zoning controls, which are

Table 6.1
Summary of Protection Options.

NONREGULATORY (VOLUNTARY) TECHNIQUES

- *Educational Initiatives*
  - *Landscape Field Guide*
  - *Interpretive Tour Guide*
  - *Roadside Pull-Offs and Interpretive Signage*
  - *Corridor Mapping*
  - *Design Manual*
  - *Property Owners Manual*
- ***Land and Easement Acquisition by a Local Land Trust***

NONREGULATORY TECHNIQUES FOR LOCAL GOVERNMENTS

Notification, Recognition, and Nonbinding Agreements
Binding Management Agreements
Incentive Programs
Technical Assistance
Designation of Historic and Scenic Corridors
Land and Easement Acquisition by a Local Government
Leaseback Arrangements for Land Management

REGULATORY TECHNIQUES FOR LOCAL GOVERNMENTS

Transfer of Development Rights
Clustering of Residential Development
Corridor Overlay Zones
Architectural and Landscape Design Review

often perceived as limiting to economic development and invasive of property rights, can be embraced as necessary to protect a community's special character.

Landscape Field Guide

A landscape field guide is the illustration and description of the component parts (characteristics) of the rural historic landscape. The objective of the field guide is to provide a framework for reading and understanding the historic patterns of land use and management that have shaped the visual character of the landscape over time. The guide should be easy to understand, educating both community residents and visitors to the region about the unique history of the area and the landscape patterns visible from the public roads that reveal that history. Distribution of the field guide to local schools, libraries, community organizations, chambers of commerce, and visitor centers could be an important step toward educating local residents and visitors about the value of the landscape as an important historical resource.

One method of preparing a field guide is described in Chapter 2 of this handbook. Other examples include *The Farm Landscape of Whatcomb County*, by Christine Carlson and Steven Durrant; and *Reading the Cultural Landscape: Ebey's Landing National Historical Reserve*, by Kathy Gilbert.

Interpretive Tour Guide

The interpretive tour guide combines elements of the field guide and the road inventory maps described in Chapter 4. The tour guide graphically details layers of regional history and landscape characteristics to the traveling public. Through a series of informative maps, motorists can learn about the natural processes, various cultures, and historical events that have shaped the visual character of the landscape over time.

A good example of an interpretive tour guide is the *Northern Kentucky Historic Back Roads Tour* by Laurie Risch and others (1992). Organized as a series of maps for an entire region, the guide highlights and describes significant historical structures, neighborhoods, districts, and related personalities. Another interesting booklet, wonderfully simple and well illustrated, is the *As We*

Were, As We Are tour guide of Woodford County Kentucky by James Rogers, Toss Chandler, and Ben Chandler. For more information about this publication, contact The Woodford County Woman's Club or the Woodford County Historical Society in Versailles, Kentucky.

Roadside Pull-Offs and Interpretive Signage

Roadside pull-offs and interpretive signs provide the traveling public with an opportunity to stop their vehicle and safely view significant landscape features. Interpretive panels with text, photos, and sketches are used to provide interesting information about the feature (historical photographs and illustrations are particulary valuable). The location of the pull-off depends on the landscape feature, safety concerns such as line of sight, and the availability of adequate space.

In Kentucky's Bluegrass region, a non-profit conservation organization has constructed several roadside pull-offs beside historic and scenic roads. The pull-offs are asphalt-paved and enclosed by board fencing that is compatible with the fencing pattern on adjacent horse farms. Information panels address both the immediate area and topics of general interest to the region. For more information contact Lexington-Frankfort Scenic Corridor, Inc. (see Appendix E).

Corridor Mapping

Based on the old adage that "one picture is worth a thousand words," presentation maps portraying graphic depictions of significant road corridors should be prepared. Maps can be used effectively to present the concept of a corridor as a significant community resource. The corridor's component parts such as the immediate roadway, the viewshed and view sequence, and ownership patterns are easily illustrated. Maps are an essential tool for presentations aimed at generating community support for road protection.

The Apalachee Land Conservancy in Tallahassee, Florida, prepared a corridor map of a locally designated "Canopy Road" that is both scenic and historically significant. Using the map as a visual aid, the land trust has successfully been able to promote the need to protect not only the immediate public right-of-way, but also the visible landscape (viewshed) to insure the preservation of the entire historic experience.

Design Manual

The design manual, in which historic and scenic landscape characteristics are described, is a logical extension of the field guide. The manual provides for the preservation of these unique components by suggesting voluntary guidelines for new developments so that projects can be constructed in a way that is compatible with historic and scenic character. Guidelines are often written for: development and access points; screening and buffering of developments; landscaping; building setbacks and placement; architecture; parking; lighting; signage; stormwater and utility infrastructure; and transportation and safety issues including accommodation of pedestrians and bicycles.

A design manual can foster greater cooperation between developers and regulators. It can also stimulate creative design solutions by presenting alternatives to the development community for enhancing and beautifying significant road corridors.

Good examples of a voluntary design manual for rural agricultural landscapes can be found in *Redland: A Preservation and Tourism Plan,* by Rocco Ceo and Margot Ammidown, and *The Farm Landscape of Whatcomb County,* by Christine Carlson and Steven Durrant.

Property Owners Manual

A property owners manual provides information about historic and scenic resources to individuals who own property within road corridors and describes goals to preserve the land. These manuals may present guidelines for making changes to property in keeping with the visual character of the region by addressing such topics as planting, signs, paving, clearing vegetation, fence designs, and rehabilitation standards for historic buildings. Information on voluntary land conservation and historic preservation techniques may also be provided.

The Lexington-Frankfort Scenic Corridor, Inc. is planning to publish a manual for individuals who own historic property between Lexington and Frankfort, Kentucky. It will be designed to provide information on: landscape protection and promotion activities; the variety of historic resources in the area; properties listed on the National Register of Historic Places; guidelines for appropriate changes to historic properties; and conservation techniques for landscape protection.

Land and Easement Acquisition by a Local Land Trust

The Land Trust Alliance defines a land trust as "a local, state, or regional non-profit organization that *directly* protects land for its natural, recreational, scenic, historic, or productive value."[11] Direct protection methods most commonly used by land trusts include acquiring land outright (fee simple) and the acquisition of conservation easements.

A *conservation easement* is a legal agreement between a landowner and easement holder that restricts the type and amount of development that can occur on the property. The easement allows for continued private ownership of the land while providing for its protection. Restrictions are tailored to the particular conditons of the property and the needs and desires of the landowner. The landowners may sell land for an easement, or make a donation and receive tax deductions on income, estate, and possibly property taxes.

The Low Country Open Land Trust in Charleston, South Carolina, has worked with landowners to place scenic easements along roads of historic and scenic significance. Low Country currently holds a one-mile long, 500-foot wide buffer easement and a 200-foot wide easement along two historic highways. In addition, they are working jointly with the National Trust for Historic Preservation to protect as much of the historic Ashley River Road as possible. For more information contact The Low Country Open Land Trust (see Appendix E).

For more information about the organization of a land trust, conservation easements, and other land conservation techniques, contact The Land Trust Alliance and The Trust for Public Land (see Appendix E).

Nonregulatory Techniques for Local Governments

Notification, Recognition, and Nonbinding Agreements

Significant resources can often be protected by notifying a landowner about the location and importance of a resource on their property. A short letter and follow-up visit by land trust or local government representative is often enough to persuade the landowner to implement protective measures. Public recognition of a landowner and their significant property with a plaque or award is a good way to instill pride. Publicity encourages resource protection because the landowner may be less likely to degrade a resource that the community has praised them for protecting. Recognition should only be bestowed with the landowner's permission. Nonbinding agreements can be negotiated privately or combined with an awards program. With this technique, the landowner signs a voluntary management agreement which stipulates long-term stewardship measures for protection of the property. The agreement is based on mutual trust, pride of ownership, and the good feelings that result from a landowner contributing to the well-being of the community. These low cost measures are not strong direct methods but they offer a good starting point for developing an effective long-term conservation program.

Binding Management Agreements

These are similar to the nonbinding agreement discussed above except that the agreement is a legally binding contract, usually for a specified period of time. These are usually temporary and work well for conservation organizations and local governments that need to buy time for implementing more permanent protection.

Incentive Programs

Tax abatements in the way of reduced property taxes have been widely used to encourage the preservation and enhancement of significant resources. Financial assistance through grants and loans is another effective type of incentive for resource protection. Many landowners would probably be happy to participate in roadside conservation activities, such as planting trees or cutting brush to open up a scenic view, if they could be reimbursed for their expenses.

Technical Assistance

Technical assistance for a range of conservation services can be provided by a local government. Resource inventories, advice on appropriate conservation measures, land management planning, and rehabilitation of historic structures are but a few of the conservation related activities that landowners may need help with in order to effectively participate in a corridor protection program.

Designation of Historic and Scenic Corridors

The designation of a road as "historic" or "scenic" is the official recognition by either a local, state, or federal agency of the significant cultural, historic, scenic, geological, or natural features within the corridor. The potency of designation as a protective measure varies depending on the authorizing legislation and the particular goals of the program.

The major goals of scenic designation often include one or more of the following: educating the public about the unique scenic, historic, cultural, and natural resources of a region; protecting and enhancing the resources within the corridor which contribute to the character of the community and its quality of life; and inducing new economic development in communities through tourism and recreation. The most important of these goals, however, is resource protection, because long-term economic benefits to the community may not be realized without it.

Designation provides the greatest protection of resources within scenic corridors when combined with strong land use and zoning regulations which require new development and other activities to be compatible with the character of the corridor. Designation is least effective when no controls are implemented to provide for the protection of historic and scenic resources.

While designation without controls, in and of itself, is not very strong, it is presented here as a viable protection measure for several reasons. Designation can be a good starting point for road protection, for it is a first step toward educating the public about the importance of significant road corridors and their contribution to the quality of life in a community or region. This type of indirect protection is less controversial than land use and zoning restrictions (which are often perceived as invasive of property rights) and thus may be easier to adopt by local governments. Stronger protection measures can be adopted in the future, after educational initiatives have achieved a strong base of community support.

Wisconsin Rustic Roads Program is widely recognized as a successful yet inexpensive scenic byway program. Administered by the Department of Transportation, it was initiated in 1973 and involves fifty-seven county, town, and municipal roads, varying in length from one to twenty-six miles each, and ranging in design from single-lane unimproved to two-lane improved roads. The only costs are for signage, promotional brochures, and a part-time program coordinator. The program has increased public respect for rural landscapes and reduced road maintenance and improvement costs. For a comprehensive review of state scenic byway designation policies and procedures contact Scenic America (see Appendix E).

The implications of official recognition to a conservation organization or a public agency are important, especially as they relate to scenic easements where the incentive of income tax benefits are an issue. Designation of a road as a scenic resource supports adjacent landowners when making the case to the Internal Revenue Service that an easement has been donated for conservation purposes, which is necessary to justify the income tax deductibility of the donation.

One example of designation leading to an effective partnership between local government and a private land trust can be found in North Florida. Leon County designated five local roads as "Canopy Roads" to recognize their scenic and historic importance to the community. To protect the lush roadside vegetation and overhanging trees the county implemented a one hundred foot setback zone on each side of the road where no development can occur and vegetation management is severely restricted. The county has no desire to implement any further regulatory measures to protect pastoral views into the landscape. However, the Apalachee Land Conservancy, a local land trust, is taking advantage of the official designation by establishing a conservation easement program which will solicit the donation of easements by adjacent landowners. The designation insures a high probability that the IRS will grant tax benefits for such donations.

Land and Easement Acquisition by a Local Government

Like a land trust, a local government can directly protect land by purchasing property in fee simple or acquiring the development rights through a conservation easement. Land acquisition is the most certain and permanent form of landscape protection. Obviously, ownership allows for better management.

Leaseback Arrangements for Land Management

Conservation land can be purchased by a local government and leased back to the previous owner or other entity subject to certain restrictions for management to protect significant resources. This arrangement provides income to the local government from the leasing arrangement and income to the land manager from agricultural or forest products or public access fees. This technique has been used successfully by the National Park Service along the Natchez Trace Parkway in Mississippi and Tennessee to preserve views over agricultural lands along this historic route. It can also be employed by local land trusts.

Regulatory Techniques for Local Governments

Transfer of Development Rights

A transfer of development rights (TDR) program restricts a landowner from building within a designated resource zone such as a scenic road corridor, but it allows him/her to sell those development rights to other landowners whose property is appropriate for development. The property and the development rights are separated, thus circumventing the problem of government "taking" by allowing the landowner to benefit monetarily by the sale of the development rights. TDR programs are notoriously difficult to administer and their use is probably limited to only the most sophisticated local governments.

Clustering of Residential Development

Clustering maintains the ratio of dwelling units to acreage but allows for the concentration of housing through smaller sized lots, thus providing for the preservation of open space. An added benefit is the possible reduction in infrastructure and construction costs. The concentration of housing into distinct nodes or units along a road can be used to preserve the open, pastoral character of a road corridor in a rural area.

Corridor Overlay Zones

Overlay zones can be designed to protect particular resources within the community, such as ridgelines, wetlands, steep slopes, and historic and scenic road corridors. For example, the scenic highway overlay in Charleston County, South Carolina, restricts signage and development and requires the preservation of vegetation within the overlay area to protect views and preserve the open character of the land.

Architectural and Landscape Design Review

Design review has been adopted by some communties to protect their aesthetic character and distinctiveness through appropriate design. Design review standards, sometimes called design guidelines, include such concepts as visual harmony and character. The design manual discussed earlier included voluntary guidelines, whereas the guidelines in design review are mandatory. Design controls are usually administered by a design review board and regulate such elements as mass, proportion, architectural features (e.g., roofs, windows, and porches), vegetation, color, texture, form, and the relationship of buildings to one another and to the roadway.

Selecting Options

The first step is to integrate potential protection options with protection programs that may already exist, such as state or local government scenic roads programs. If these programs are in place, determine if the study area roads are eligible for designation. At the outset of the study, contact the local road department or the state department of transportation for information on their protection programs (if any). Also, review city and county ordinances which might apply to the protection of historic and scenic roads. Local comprehensive plans, if any, should be reviewed to determine existing protection measures. Refer to sections of the plan describing transportation, the environment, conservation, open space, or historic preservation for policies which may provide protection for road corridors.

If new or additional types of protection are necessary, develop a set of selection criteria to help guide decisions. The criteria should reinforce protection goals and objectives (i.e., resource recognition, protection and promotion, and tourism and economic development), as well as reflect the relative historic and scenic value of the road determined through the evaluation process of Chapter 5. For example, protection techniques for roads ranked as "highly significant" may require regulatory measures such as protective zoning designation to preserve and maintain the existing character of the corridor, while roads of lower significance might benefit from nonregulatory incentive programs aimed at enhancing the visual environment.

Additional selection criteria might include: (1) the number of roads that will be included in the program; (2) the degree of community interest and support; (3) the degree of support by local officials; (4) the costs of implementation; (5) staffing needs for the administering agencies and/or organizations; and (6) the degree to which the road is threatened by changes which could degrade the historic and scenic environment.

Corridor Management Planning

Whether applying one or two protection measures or the entire range of alternatives, plans should be devised for managing the study area corridors. Although an ideal corridor management plan combines land use and zoning regulations, nonregulatory measures such as incentive programs, and voluntary techniques, plans that are less comprehensive can also be effective. The plan should address each corridor separately and include both the public domain (roadway and rights-of-way) and the adjacent visible landscape (viewshed).

Corridor management planning includes: (1) reviewing project goals and objectives regarding the historic and scenic resources along the corridor; (2) determining the most appropriate and feasible protection options to meet the objectives; (3) implementing the protection options; and (4) monitoring and revising the plan periodically as other protection options may become available. Management planning is most effective when government agencies, business organizations, conservation organizations, community groups, and landowners work in partnership to implement a range of creative techniques and solutions.

Unfortunately, there are few good examples of successfully implemented corridor management plans, though some communities and regions are on the right track. There are also some recent publications mentioned below which describe the process of corridor management planning in detail.

Three counties and nine municipalities in rural west Georgia are working with the Chattahoochee-Flint Regional Development Center (RDC) to implement a heritage corridor plan along 56 miles of highway within an hour's drive of metro Atlanta. The RDC (a regional planning agency) organized a steering committee of local preservationists, chambers of commerce, and interested citizens to formulate long-term management goals for the corridor. By consensus, *economic development through tourism* and *historic and scenic resource protection and enhancement* were adopted as the major goals of the plan. The RDC is currently conducting a detailed inventory of the corridor which will be used by the steering committee to develop a host of strategies and techniques to achieve the corridor goals. It is anticipated that the steering committee will evolve into a more structured non-profit organization to oversee the implemenatation of the plan (see Appendix E for Chattahoochee-Flint Regional Development Center).

In Tallahassee, Florida, the Tallahassee City Commission and Leon County Commission have jointly adopted a canopy roads management plan. In 1991, the commissions asked a volunteer committee of concerned citizens to develop a cost-effective plan for the protection, improvement, maintenance, and expansion of the canopy road system—five officially recognized historic and scenic roads characterized by dense overhanging liveoaks and other hardwood trees creating a unique tunnel-like effect that dates back to the Antebellum Period. The Canopy Roads Citizens Committee, with the assistance of Tallahassee-Leon County Planning Department staff, inventoried the roads to describe the condition of the roadside vegetation, especially the condition of the canopy trees. Based on the inventory, management units were delineated and assigned a management objective depending on the condition of the tree canopy. The objective of maintenance was assigned to high quality canopy, enhancement to medium quality canopy, and restoration to low quality canopy. Finally, a set of vegetation management activities (techniques) was prescribed for each management unit to accomplish the specific objective. These prescriptions form the basis of the canopy road work plan which is currently being implemented in a one hundred foot setback zone on each side of the road. (See Bibliography entry for Canopy Roads Citizens Committee 1992.)

Scenic America, a nonprofit organization dedicated to preserving and enhancing the scenic character of America's communities and countryside, recently produced *Preparing Corridor Management Plans: A Scenic Byways Guidebook* for the Federal Highway Administration. Although this manual is intended to aid states in the development of corridor management plans which are required for all national scenic byways and all-American roads nominations, it should also be useful to communities for protecting historic and scenic roads of local and regional significance. (See Appendix E: Scenic America.)

As a companion volume to Scenic America's publication, the National Trust for Historic Preservation prepared a guidebook for citizen involvement in corridor management planning. The primary purpose of the *Community Guide to Corridor Management Planning for Scenic Byways* is to assist individuals, community organizations, and local governments in pursuing the opportunities of scenic byway designation and corridor management at any level. (See Appendix E: National Trust for Historic Preservation.)

Red Hills Case Study

A major objective in the Red Hills was to propose a historic and scenic byway system for the Red Hills region. The byway system is intended to meet the major goals of the study by enhancing public awareness of and appreciation for the special landscape resources of the Red Hills and by initiating a process for protecting the historic and scenic attributes of the region's rural roads.

The initial design is composed of four roads that, together, provide a variety of historical and scenic experiences. These roads should serve as the framework for a system which can be expanded in the future as need arises and interest grows.

Following the assumption that education is fundamental to the protection of rural landscapes, the proposed byways will serve as the basis for an interpretive guide. The guide is intended to reveal the region's layers of history and landscape characteristics to the traveling public. Through a series of informative maps, motorists can learn about the natural processes, various cultures, and historical events that have shaped the visual character of this unique landscape over time.

Historic and Scenic Byways of the Red Hills

Based on the evaluation and guidance from the Red Hills Conservation Association, the following roads were selected for the initial byway design:

- US 319 (Thomasville Road)
- Meridian Road
- Beachton-Metcalf Road
- New Hope Road

The network, as illustrated in Figure 6.1, provides a diversity of travel experiences and visual access to a variety of historic and scenic resources. Featured roads are,

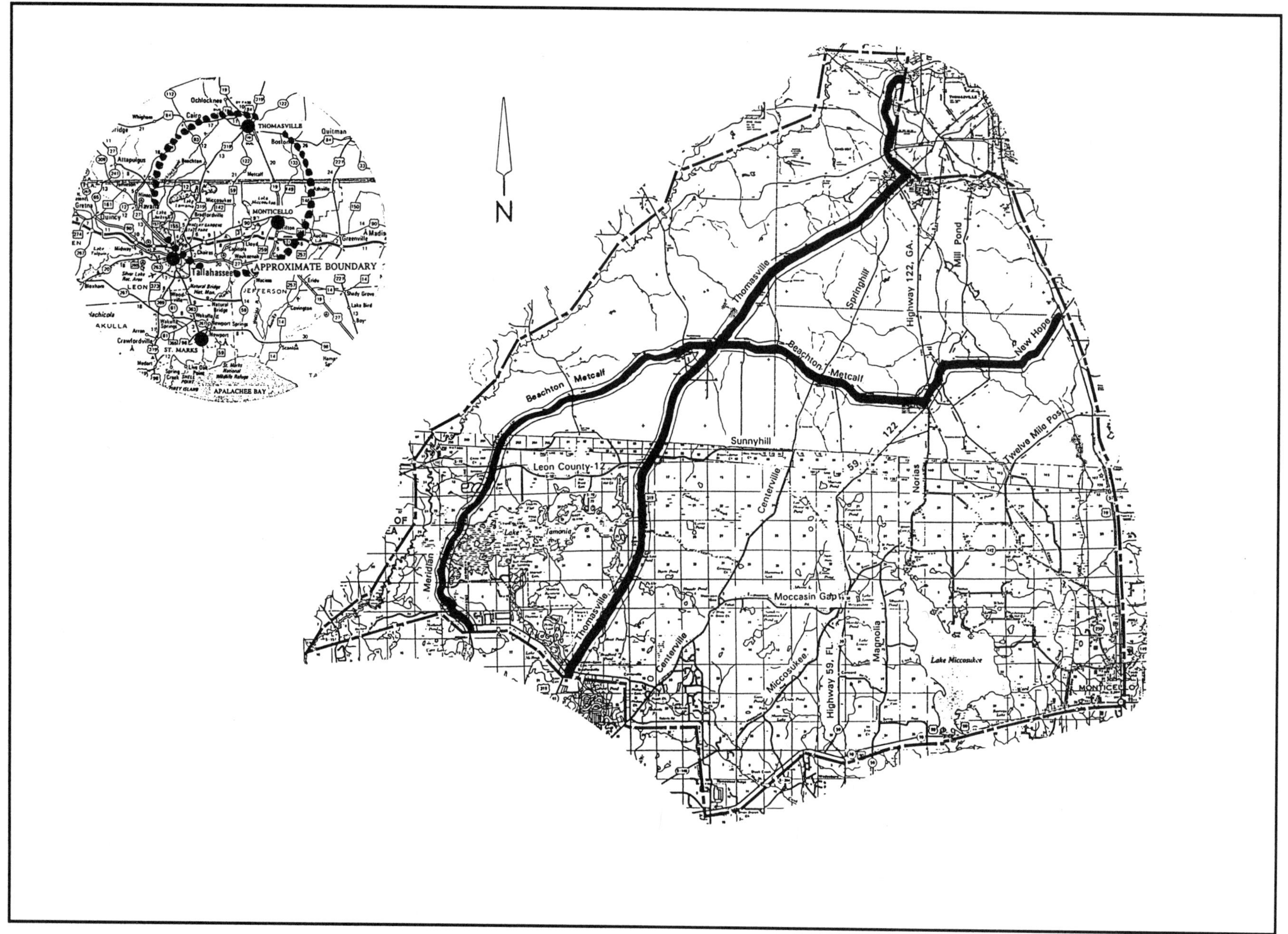

Figure 6.1 *Proposed Historic and Scenic Byways of the Red Hills.*

for the most part, well traveled, addressing the concerns of landowners that the inclusion of remote roads could attract too many sightseers, leading to the destruction of the historic and scenic qualities that make the roads so special. The proposed network provides important linkages through the region. The north to south and east to west configuration through the very heart of the plantation belt provides a strategic framework of roads which, if protected by a combination of regulatory and voluntary measures, would contribute significantly toward the preservation of the integrity of the quail plantation region.

The Interpretive Guide

Today, the landscape integrity of the Red Hills is threatened. Fragmentation of the area is already underway as suburbs expand from Tallahassee and Thomasville. Rural roads are being widened and paved, and gas and electric utilities have targeted the region for potential transmission corridor construction.

The historical and ecological significance of the Red Hills has, for the most part, gone unnoticed by the general public, and this only adds to the region's vulnerability. The protection and preservation of special landscapes is only possible if they are valued by the public at large. The voting public will support the Red Hills Conservation Initiative only if they are aware of and value this region's special resources. Education is therefore the basis for public counteraction when threats to the integrity of the landscape become imminent.

The purpose of the interpretive guide is to educate the public about the Red Hill's fascinating natural and cultural history. The intent is to make it clear that the sequence of visual images experienced along the roads is, in fact, a record of history. Understanding the ecological and cultural patterns of the landscape then adds meaning and depth to the scenery. In this way the region's roads become a point of departure for learning about the qualities which contribute to the uniqueness of the Red Hills.

The interpretive guide (Fig. 6.2), based on the proposed byway system, is composed of a series of maps and narrative sheets.

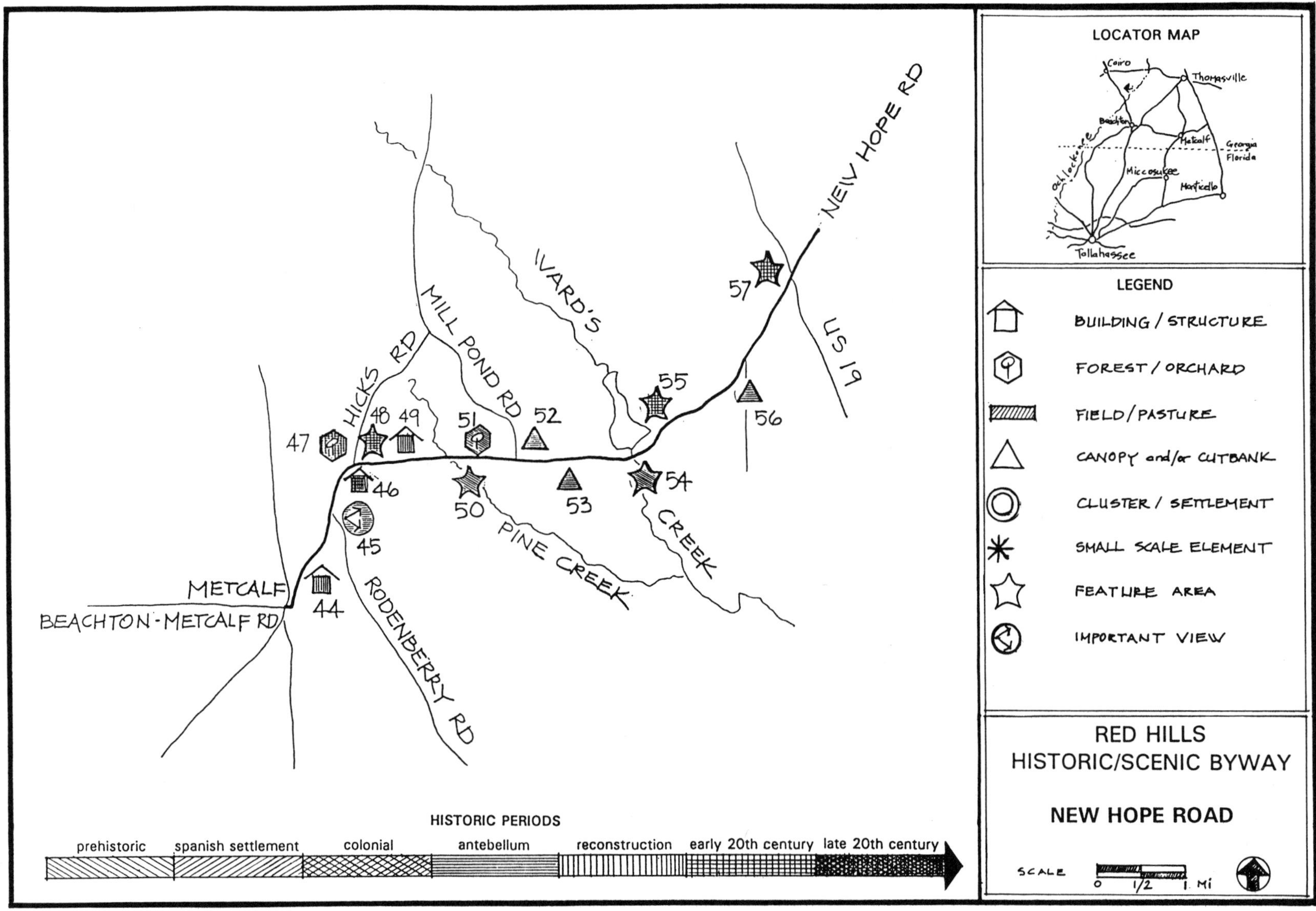

Figure 6.2 *Interpretive Tour Guide for New Hope Road, Thomas County, Georgia. (Note that color codings were converted to patterns for reproduction in this handbook.)*

New Hope Road begins directly northeast of Metcalf and winds its way northward fourteen miles to its intersection with US 84 and Five Forks Road. The lower portion of New Hope Road (6.7 miles) is the most historic and scenic segment of the roadway. The road gets its name from New Hope Church which has records dating back to 1851. The church stood at the northwest corner of the intersection of New Hope and Thomasville-Monticello Road (US 19). This historic route was a main line road linking Tallahassee to Metcalf, Boston, Barwick, Pavo and points north in Georgia.

44. **TENANT CABINS** once dotted the landscape. They were characterized by square construction with a shed roofed porch in the front, brick fireplace with exterior chimney, vertical plank doors, window shutters, no window glass, and weatherboard siding. Inadequate cooking facilities, overcrowding, with no indoor plumbing characterized the substandard living conditions experienced by many tenant families after the Civil War and well into the Twentieth Century.

45. Today, this beautiful canopy road, with its hard baked clay surface, contains some of the most scenic views in the region. The road begins on a high ridge, providing a **PANORAMIC VIEW** eastward of Holly Hill Plantation. This view reveals large fields bordered by pines and a large pecan grove. Holly Hill, a small estate of 791 acres as compared to the larger hunting properties, is meticulously maintained.

The large field pattern visible here provides a clue to the visual character of the antebellum landscape which was dominated by extensive fields of cotton and corn.

46. **HOLLY HILL PLANTATION ENTRY DRIVE AND MANAGER'S RESIDENCE**

47. **PECAN ORCHARDS** represent the efforts of area farmers around the turn of the century to diversify cash crops in the region.

48. As the road proceeds eastward the **HICKS FAMILY CEMETERY**, dating to the turn of the century, is located around the bend at the corner of New Hope and Hicks Road.

49. **TENANT CABIN**

50. Drainages such as **PINE CREEK** serve as natural firebreaks in pinelands which are burned annually, usually late winter, to maintain a productive habitat for quail.

51. This **STAND OF LONGLEAF PINE** is managed by the principles set forth by Herbert Stoddard in the 1930's. He advocated selective cutting to improve the appearance and quality of the forest while at the same time enhancing wildlife values. Today Stodddard's principles are carried out by Mr. Leon Neel who is the forestry consultant for many of the quail plantations in Georgia.

52. To a large degree, the 7 mile **MILL POND ROAD** to Thomasville could be considered a private plantation road, as both sides are surrounded by hunting estates. Like New Hope Road, Mill Pond Road conveys the scenic experience of a private drive through the middle of these great hunting plantations. The narrow dirt road is bordered by park-like pine forest and small patch fields. Other segments contain columns of stately live oaks forming a green canopy.

Two overpasses on Mill Pond Road were designed by Warren Manning as part of a larger landscaping project for Millpond Plantation. Manning collaborated with Frederick Law Olmsted in the design of the Biltmore gardens in Asheville, North Carolina. Spanning 32 feet, these wood plank and steel girder **BRIDGES** still enable hunting wagons to pass over Mill Pond Road.

53. New Hope Road contains a unique, **PRISTINE CANOPY** section just east of Mill Pond Road. Under the cathedral-like setting, the eighteen foot dirt road makes a series of curves around majestic live oaks. No other canopy road in the region has such curves, and no attempt has been made to straighten the road as it swerves around these beautiful trees. A distinguished sense of place on this old wagon road is experienced. This road was not cut for the automobile. High clay embankments, reaching almost eight feet, attest to this.

54. While most drainage in the Red Hills is underground, **WARD'S CREEK** is one of the major surface streams in the region, flowing some 20 miles from Thomasville into Lake Miccosukee.

55. **SEDGEFIELD PLANTATION**. The subtle wrought-iron entry sign and handsome farm complex of forest green barns and white foreman's house is in clear view of the road.

56. The **PLANTED LIVE OAK CANOPY DRIVE** to the Greenwood plantation main house reflects an earlier antebellum tradition.

57. At the intersection with US 19, a concrete block grocery store and Bar-B-Q stands south of the road. According to its current owner, the store was built shortly after World War II. Most likely it replaced an earlier store, as this **CROSSROADS LOCATION** was an active place. Besides the New Hope Church, just up US 19 was the black Bethel Church and school. By 1939, a number of dwellings formed a small crossroad village. Today, only the Bar-B-Q remains. But at the southeast corner of the crossroads, a roadside park, possibly constructed under the New Deal's WPA, still greets visitors.

253 254

Figure 6.2 (*continued*)

Each road was mapped and important landscape characteristics within the corridor were located by a particular symbol. With a number, each symbol was keyed to a descriptive phrase on an accompanying text sheet. The brief narratives provide only a basic level of information about landscape characteristics. Finally, the symbols were color-coded according to the historic period(s) with which the characteristic is associated. The intent is to provide a broad overview of natural and historical processes that have shaped the character of the region over time. An atlas format was chosen due to its ease of use in a moving automobile.

Bluegrass Case Study

Presented below are the corridor management planning steps for Old Frankfort and Pisgah Pikes. Steps 1 through 3 were conducted at the third and final Scenic Advisory Panel meeting. Steps 4 and 5—"implementation of the plan" and "monitoring and revising the plan" have not yet been conducted but will hopefully be accomplished over time. This process builds on Bluegrass case study material presented in previous chapters.

Review Goals and Objectives

Management goals were defined at the outset of the Bluegrass case study by posing a series of questions to the Scenic Advisory Panel: What is the desired outcome of long term management? Do you want to protect the historic and scenic resources? Do you want to promote those resources by publicly recognizing them? For Old Frankfort Pike and Pisgah Pike, the goals of preservation, improvement, and protection of the scenic character were identified.

The study team identified three management objectives for each preference category: maintenance, enhancement, and restoration/creation (see case study in Chapter 3). For "high preference" views (Category One), *maintenance* was selected to preserve the present features of the existing viewshed. For "medium preference" views (Category Two), *enhancement* was chosen to improve upon the present physical/perceptual quality of the viewshed. For "low preference" views in Category Three, *restoration and/or creation* was selected to establish conditions more in keeping with the historic fabric of the Bluegrass landscape (Fig. 6.3).

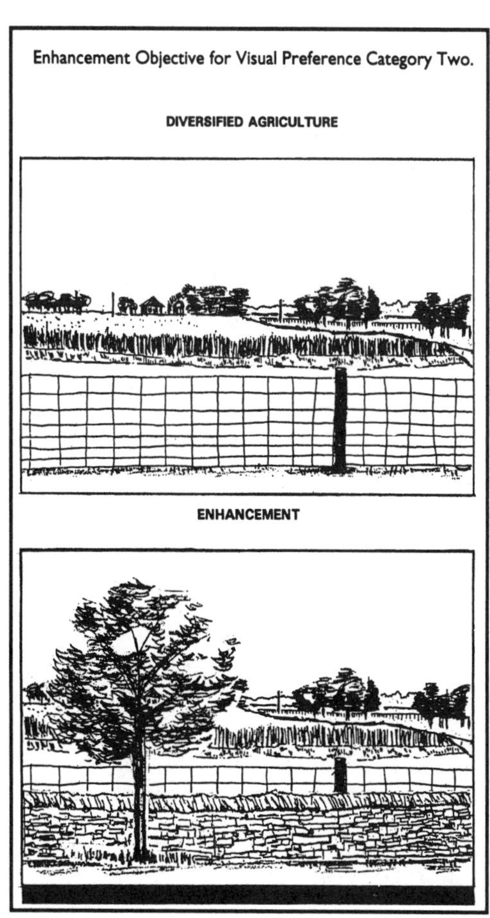

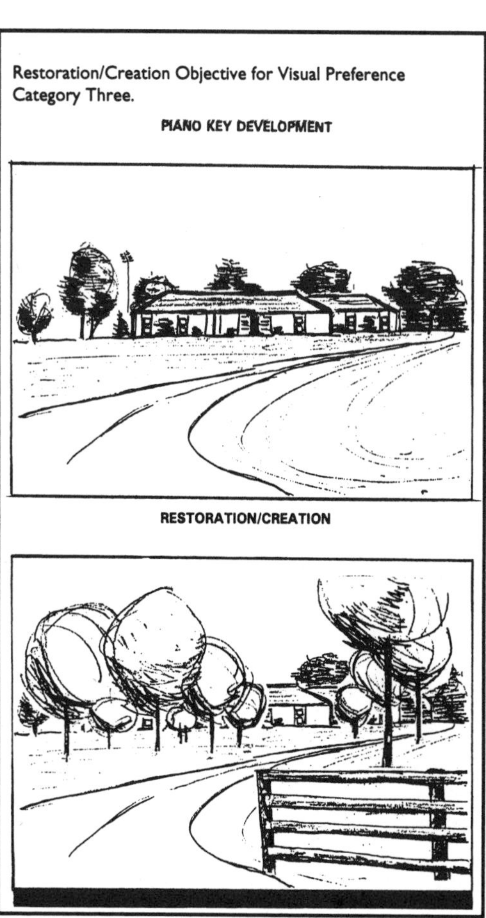

Figure 6.3 *Management Objectives, as Applied to the Visual Preference Categories in the Bluegrass Case Study.*

Once identified, the Scenic Advisory Panel reviewed and approved the study team's definitions and application of the objectives to the preference categories. The study team then applied the appropriate objective to each management unit within the two corridors (Fig. 6.4).

Applying objectives to each management unit facilitates the assessment of priority areas along a corridor. For example, maintenance and enhancement zones may warrant long-term, low-intensity considerations, while restoration/creation zones may become the focus of more immediate efforts.

Explore Protection Options

The Scenic Advisory Panel was asked to participate in a brainstorming exercise to generate a list of possible protection strategies and techniques for three different preference categories and related management objectives.

Slides illustrating views from each of the preference categories (high, medium, and low) were shown to the panel, who were asked to list as many protection options for that particular type of view possible. Their list was then reorganized by the project team into regulatory, non-regulatory, and voluntary techniques, which took approximately one hour (Table 6.2).

Select Appropriate Strategies and Techniques

The Scenic Advisory Panel was asked to select from the list of options the most appropriate strategies and techniques and to apply them to management units along the road corridors. The study team distributed four maps, each representing one of four distinct road segments, and asked the panel to work in teams of three or four. Panel members were encouraged to work on a segment of the road with which they were very familiar. Using the panel's maps, the study team developed a draft work plan. Figure 6.5 illustrates the work plan developed for one segment of Old Frankfort Pike. Table 6.3 is a list of management prescriptions as applied to all road segments in the study.

The work plan is composed of a set of prescriptions to achieve the stated objective for each management unit. The prescriptions primarily identify

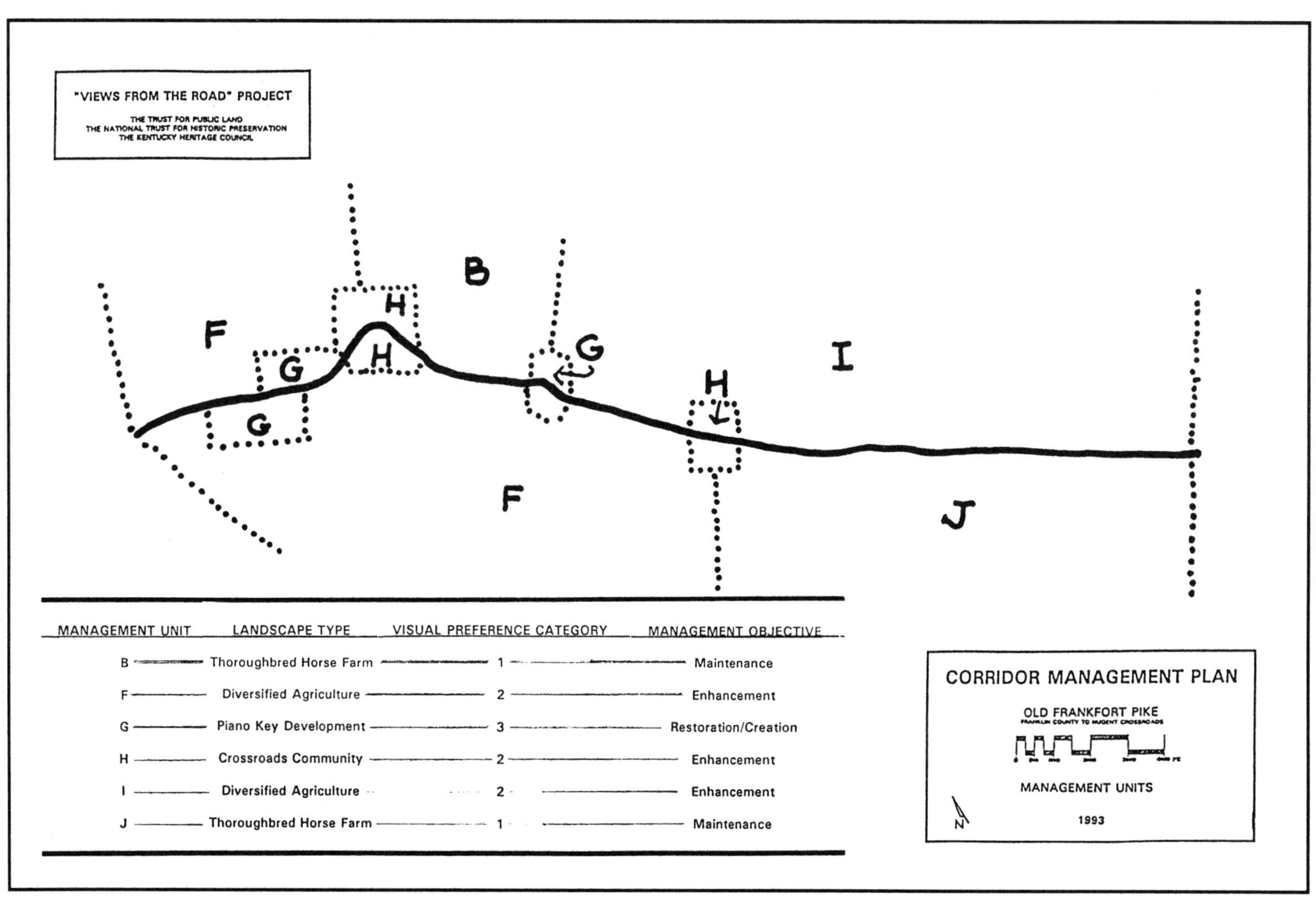

Figure 6.4 *Management Objectives, as Applied to Management Units along a Segment of Old Frankfort Pike, Bluegrass Case Study.*

Regulatory Measures

Designate roads as historic and scenic and establish corridor overlay zone. Within overlay zone implement the following measures:

Thirty acre minimum lot size along Old Frankfort Pike Corridor in Fayette County.
Sign ordinance and billboard control.
Design guidelines to set standards for the siting of new buildings within viewsheds.

Establish design standards for Kentucky Department of Transportation realignments and bridge replacements.

Establish tree pruning standards for transmission line maintenance.

Establish inter-local government agreements between Fayette County Urban Government and Woodford County to implement measures listed above.

Non-Regulatory Measures

Implement scenic easement program to protect corridor viewshed.

Establish roadside vegetation management program to include:

Canopy trees - species selection, planting patterns, maintenance requirements.
Hedgerows - species selection, planting patterns, maintenance requirements.
Wildflowers - species selection, planting patterns, maintenance requirements.
Sod Verges - mowing regimes.
Training for roadside maintenance crews in the application of appropriate vegetation management techniques.
Grants to private landowners for managing vegetation as specified in the corridor management plan.

Establish rock fence/wall preservation program including:

Vocational training for local artisans in traditional stonework techniques.
Grants to private landowners for restoring, reconstructing, and maintaining stone fences and walls.
Establish preservation program for historic buildings and structures including:
Vocational training for local artisans in traditional construction techniques.
Grants to private landowners for restoring, reconstructing, and maintaining historic buildings and structures.

Establish savanna woodland preservation program including:

Development of management techniques and specifications (species selection, planting patterns, maintenance requirements).
Training for land managers in management techniques.
Provision of grants to private landowners for restoring and maintaining savanna woodland remnants.
Establishment of a conservation easement acquisition program by local government and land trust.

Develop educational programs.

Present the corridor management planning program to local residents, especially landowners along roadways. Describe significant resources.

Establish neighborhood/community landscape awards program.

Acknowledge the stewardship practices of landowners who manage their lands in ways that protect and preserve the integrity of the scenic roads.

Conduct a feasibility study to determine the cost of placing transmission lines underground. Compare cost to that of long-term maintenance of lines above ground. Install transmission lines underground where feasible.

Voluntary Measures

Implement land management practices that contribute the visual character of the road corridors.

Donate or sell land or easements (as identified on the corridor management plan) to local government or land trust.

Manage roadside vegetation as specified in corridor management plan.

Restore and preserve woodland savanna remnants.

Restore and preserve rock walls/fences.

Restore and preserve historic buildings and structures.

Make cash contributions to local governments and/or land trusts to implement elements of the corridor management plan.

Inform neighbors of corridor management planning program and its benefits.

Table 6.2 *Protection Options Developed by the Bluegrass Scenic Advisory Panel for Pisgah Pike and Old Frankfort Pike.*

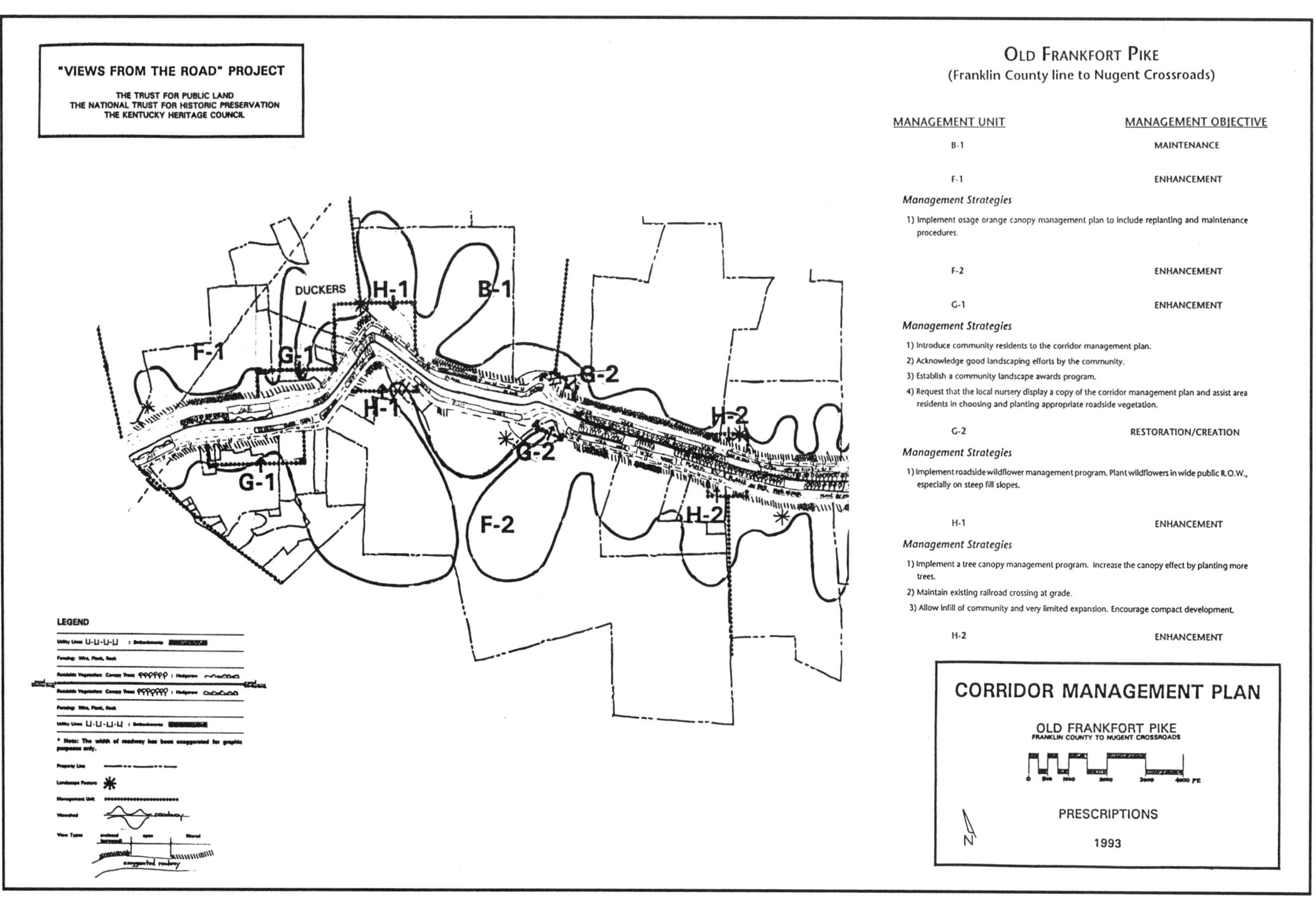

Figure 6.5 *Draft Work Plan Developed by the Bluegrass Scenic Advisory Panel for a Segment of Old Frankfort Pike.*

Pisgah Pike

MANAGEMENT UNIT	MANAGEMENT OBJECTIVE
A-1	ENHANCEMENT

Management Strategies

1) Implement a canopy tree management program. Plant more trees to increase density of roadside canopy.
2) Plant shrubs and small trees to increase density of understory vegetation along road.

A-2	ENHANCEMENT

Management Strategies

1) Implement osage orange hedge management program to include replanting and maintenance procedures.
2) Extend existing osage orange hedges.
3) Implement osage orange canopy management program to include replanting and maintenance procedures.
4) Extend existing osage orange canopy.

A-3	ENHANCEMENT

Management Strategies

1) Implement a tree canopy management program. Plant more trees to increase density of roadside canopy. Extend sycamore tree canopy.
2) Remove white tin strip on top of wire fencing.
3) Implement woodland savanna management program to include reforestation and maintenance. Plant burr oak and blue ash.
4) Implement rock fence/wall management program to include restoration and maintenance.

Table 6.3 *Management Prescriptions as Applied to the Work Plan for Pisgah Pike and Old Frankfort Pike by the Bluegrass Scenic Advisory Panel.*

Pisgah Pike

MANAGEMENT UNIT	MANAGEMENT OBJECTIVE
B-1	MAINTENANCE

MANAGEMENT UNIT	MANAGEMENT OBJECTIVE
B-2	RESTORATION/CREATION

Management Strategies

1) Screen castle with dense planting of trees and shrubs.

MANAGEMENT UNIT	MANAGEMENT OBJECTIVE
B-3	MAINTENANCE

Management Strategies

1) Repair and maintain plank fences.

MANAGEMENT UNIT	MANAGEMENT OBJECTIVE
C-1	MAINTENANCE

Management Strategies

1) Plant trees to filter views of brick barn (incompatible architecture).
2) Implement an osage orange canopy management program. Remove evergreen trees from osage orange canopy and replant with osage orange.

MANAGEMENT UNIT	MANAGEMENT OBJECTIVE
C-2	MAINTENANCE

Management Strategies

1) Implement woodland savanna management program to include reforestation and maintenance. Plant burr oak and blue ash.
2) Paint horse barn a more harmonious color.
3) Screen house trailer.

Table 6.3 (*continued*)

Pisgah Pike

MANAGEMENT UNIT	MANAGEMENT OBJECTIVE
D-1	ENHANCEMENT
E-1	MAINTENANCE
F-1	ENHANCEMENT

Management Strategies

1) Plant trees to filter view of modern brick home.

MANAGEMENT UNIT	MANAGEMENT OBJECTIVE
F-2	ENHANCEMENT
F-3	ENHANCEMENT

Management Strategies

1) Maintain long views.
2) Maintain beautiful view of Pisgah Manse.

Table 6.3 (*continued*)

OLD FRANKFORT PIKE
(Franklin County line to Nugent Crossroads)

MANAGEMENT UNIT	MANAGEMENT OBJECTIVE
B-1	MAINTENANCE
F-1	ENHANCEMENT

Management Strategies

1) Implement osage orange canopy management plan to include replanting and maintenance procedures.

MANAGEMENT UNIT	MANAGEMENT OBJECTIVE
F-2	ENHANCEMENT
G-1	ENHANCEMENT

Management Strategies

1) Introduce community residents to the corridor management plan.
2) Acknowledge good landscaping efforts by the community.
3) Establish a community landscape awards program.
4) Request that the local nursery display a copy of the corridor management plan and assist area residents in choosing and planting appropriate roadside vegetation.

MANAGEMENT UNIT	MANAGEMENT OBJECTIVE
G-2	RESTORATION/CREATION

Management Strategies

1) Implement roadside wildflower management program. Plant wildflowers in wide public R.O.W., especially on steep fill slopes.

Table 6.3 (*continued*)

Old Frankfort Pike
(Franklin County line to Nugent Crossroads)

MANAGEMENT UNIT	MANAGEMENT OBJECTIVE
H-1	ENHANCEMENT

Management Strategies

1) Implement a tree canopy management program. Increase the canopy effect by planting more trees.
2) Maintain existing railroad crossing at grade.
3) Allow infill of community and very limited expansion. Encourage compact development.

MANAGEMENT UNIT	MANAGEMENT OBJECTIVE
H-2	ENHANCEMENT
I-1	MAINTENANCE

Management Strategies

1) Implement woodland savanna management program to include reforestation and maintenance procedures.
2) Implement rock fence/wall management program to include restoration and maintenance. Protect rock walls by installing new fences on the private property side of the rock wall.
3) Implement a tree canopy management plan to include reforestation and maintenance.

MANAGEMENT UNIT	MANAGEMENT OBJECTIVE
J-1	MAINTENANCE

Management Strategies

1) Implement a tree canopy management program to include reforestation and maintenance.

Table 6.3 (*continued*)

OLD FRANKFORT PIKE
(Nugent Crossroads to Faywood)

MANAGEMENT UNIT	MANAGEMENT OBJECTIVE
B-1	MAINTENANCE

Management Strategies

1) Selectively plant groups of trees along roadway to add interest. A canopy effect is not intended for this section.
2) Selectively plant groups of trees in the middleground and background, especially on ridgeline.

MANAGEMENT UNIT	MANAGEMENT OBJECTIVE
B-2	MAINTENANCE
C-1	MAINTENANCE
E-1	MAINTENANCE
F-1	ENHANCEMENT

Management Strategies

1) Acknowledge good stewardship practices of diversified farmers. Introduce farmers to the corridor management plan and request their cooperation.

MANAGEMENT UNIT	MANAGEMENT OBJECTIVE
F-2	ENHANCEMENT

Management Strategies

1) Continue tree plantings along interfarm fence boundaries.
2) Acknowledge good stewardship practices of diversified farmers. Introduce farmers to the corridor management plan and request their cooperation.

MANAGEMENT UNIT	MANAGEMENT OBJECTIVE
F-3	ENHANCEMENT

Management Strategies

1) Replant trees in front of Mt. Vernon Church
2) Repair fences

Table 6.3 (*continued*)

Old Frankfort Pike
(Nugent Crossroads to Faywood)

MANAGEMENT UNIT	MANAGEMENT OBJECTIVE
G-1	RESTORATION/CREATION

Management Strategies

1) Plant trees and hedges along roadway to create a more compatible look for piano key lots.
2) Plant trees and hedges along private driveways to create a more compatible look for piano key lots.

H-1	ENHANCEMENT

Management Strategies

1) Screen trailer park with dense plantings of trees and shrubs on private lots and along roadside.
2) Renovate stores and other structures to appropriate styles. Utilize tax credits.

K-1	RESTORATION/CREATION

Management Strategies

1) Encourage infill and compact development.

L-1	MAINTENANCE

Management Strategies

1) Develop design standards for siting new development.
2) Selectively plant tree groupings along roadside. Canopy effect is not intended here. 3) Selectively plant tree groupings in barren pasture especially on ridgelines.

M-1	ENHANCEMENT

Management Strategies

1) Discuss the improvement of property management with absentee landowner to enhance views from the road.
2) Implement woodland savanna management program, especially along creek which parallels Old Frankfort Pike.

Table 6.3 (*continued*)

Old Frankfort Pike
(Faywood to Viley Road)

MANAGEMENT UNIT	MANAGEMENT OBJECTIVE
B-1	MAINTENANCE

Management Strategies

1) Place transmission lines underground along Old Frankfort Pike in Fayette County.
2) Selectively plant tree groupings along roadside to add interest and to filter views of utility poles, especially on hilltop locations. Be careful to preserve the open quality of the landscape and important long views.
3) Implement sign control ordinance (Fayette County Urban Government).

B-2	MAINTENANCE

Management Strategies

1) Maintain no fence zone as indicated on the plan. This zone creates a pleasing contrast to a roadside which is almost totally dominated by fencing.
2) Implement a stone wall/fence management program near Viley Road intersection. Include measures for restoration and maintenance.
3) Implement woodland savanna management program on property directly across from Little property. Include measures for reforestation and maintenance.
4) Seek a conservation easement over the Little property, especially in gateway area.
5) Implement a woodland savanna management program on Little property at intersection of Viley Road.

F-1	ENHANCEMENT

Management Strategies

1) Negotiate with landowner to relocate barracks.
2) Plant trees along roadside to filter views of barracks in the interim.

M-1	MAINTENANCE

Table 6.3 (*continued*)

management strategies. Specific steps or techniques to achieve the strategies remain to be completed. For example, rock wall restoration is recommended for certain management units, but construction standards, specifications, and costs are yet to be developed. The same is true for all of the incentive programs listed in Table 6.3, such as roadside tree planting, woodland savanna restoration, and roadside wildflower planting.

Implementation of the Plan

Funding for many of the prescriptions specified in this plan will ultimately decide whether or not they are implemented. Available funding sources should be explored, including private foundations, nonprofit organizations, and public agencies. One of the most promising sources for funding of highway corridor enhancement projects is Federal Highway Administration money available through the Intermodal Surface Transportation Efficiency Act (ISTEA) of 1991. The Scenic Advisory Panel should contact the The Kentucky Transportation Cabinet, The Kentucky Heritage Council, and local metropolitan planning organizations for information and instructions on applying for "ISTEA Enhancement Funds."

It is recommended that the Bluegrass Scenic Advisory Panel advocate the funding and implementation of management prescriptions through a series of public meetings in the study area. The meetings are intended to solicit the support, cooperation, and participation of local landowners, public agencies, community groups, and conservation and preservation organizations. Community involvement and commitment is essential for accomplishing the goals and objectives of the plan.

Monitor and Revise the Plan

The management plan will have to be monitored over the long term to assess the effects of the management prescriptions. As prescriptions are implemented within the corridors, updates should be made to the plan from year to year so that progress and setbacks can be recorded. A thorough review of the plan should be conducted at least every five years so that the inevitable modifications and refinements can be made.

Conclusion

The aim of this handbook is to help communities integrate the visual and aesthetic qualities of rural road corridors with the history of land use to provide a rational basis for public and private land conservation efforts. The process presented here represents a sequence of steps for identifying significant historic landscape characteristics and scenic resources and developing measures for their preservation and enhancement. This method offers a good starting point for protecting rural landscapes, but it must be emphasized that it is only a beginining. The handbook does not deal with the larger economic, demographic, and political issues which must be addressed in order to develop a larger comprehensive land protection plan.

In all rural areas there are a variety of resources that may warrant protection and a range of tools that are available to protect these resources. However, it is ultimately the commitment of individuals to *act* that is vital to the success of countryside preservation efforts. This commitment by the people who know and love their community is often the missing ingredient. This handbook is intended to encourage not only those citizens but also community groups and local governments in their efforts to protect and enhance *views from the road.*

APPENDICES

APPENDIX A

SAMPLE LETTERS OF INVITATION TO THE SCENIC ADVISORY PANEL

Dear Mr. Goodview:

It is with great pleasure that I write to request your participation on a Scenic Advisory Panel for a rural roads study presently underway in the Red Hills region of North Florida and South Georgia. The project is being carried out by The Trust for Public Land and The Red Hills Conservation Association for the purpose of determining the historic and scenic significance of the network of public roads in the region. This type of information is critical for planning protection strategies for the unique visual experiences along these roads. The proposed panel, a cross section of Red Hills residents, has been recommended by the Red Hills Conservation Association because of their familiarity with the area. Your insights will contribute significantly to this study of the scenic qualities of the beautiful country roads in the Red Hills.

The Scenic Advisory Panel is a steering committee that will act as a compass. It will direct the efforts of the study team by helping us:

- define and locate the different types of visual experiences that exist along the network of public roads, and
- confirm that video samples accurately represent these defined areas.

These "road experience" types, represented in a video format, will then be used to determine the visual preferences of the public at large. Information collected from this part of the study can be used to plan protection strategies and management plans for those special rural roads which are perceived as the most scenic.

As a member of the Scenic Advisory Panel, you will be asked to attend three meetings (7 p.m. to 9 p.m.) scheduled for Wednesday June 10, Wednesday June 24, 1992, and a date in August to be determined. The first two meetings are critical and require your participation. However, if you have a conflict, we may be able to reschedule. The final meeting will be a presentation by the study team of their findings on the public perspectives and preferences for certain road experience types, as defined by the Scenic Advisory Panel.

The location of the first and second meetings is in Tallahassee at the Brokaw-McDougall House (see the enclosed map). The location of the third meeting will be announced later.

If you are interested in participating in this exciting project to define and protect scenic byways in the Red Hills, please contact David Copps at The Trust for Public Land in Tallahassee, Florida (904/422-1404) no later than Monday, June 1st. Thank you for your consideration of this invitation. I look forward to hearing from you soon.

Sincerely,
David Copps
Project Associate
Southeast Region

May 21, 1992
Sally Scenery
123 Buena Vista Drive
Versailles, KY.

Dear Mrs. Scenery:

It is with great pleasure that I write to request your participation on a local Scenic Advisory Panel for The Kentucky Heritage Council's "Views from the Road" project. Under a grant from the National Trust for Historic Preservation and with the support of the Trust for Public Land, we are requesting your assistance to help us determine the historic and scenic significance of public roads in the Bluegrass region. A fact sheet is enclosed explaining this landscape protection effort in greater detail.

You were recommended to us by the ____________________ because of your knowledge of and concern about the Bluegrass. We would like you to serve on our Scenic Advisory Panel for the Bluegrass rural roads study presently underway as part of our "Views from the Road" Project.

The Scenic Advisory Panel will act as a compass for the study. The panel will direct the efforts of the study team to help define and locate the different types of visual experiences that exist along the public roads in the Bluegrass.

We are requesting approximately six hours of your time to give your input about the historic and scenic qualities of the roads in the region. We have tentatively scheduled three two-hour panel meetings (from 7:00 p.m. to 9:00 p.m.) on Thursday October 8, Thursday October 22, 1992, and a date in November to be determined to complete our work. The location of the meetings will be in Frankfort at the ______________ House, _______________ Street (see the enclosed map).

The Kentucky Heritage Council and the Trust for Public Land believes the type of information this project will provide is critical for planning protection strategies for the outstanding scenic beauty of the Bluegrass. Your unique insights—and those of your fellow panel members—will contribute significantly to this study of the scenic qualities of the beautiful country roads in the Bluegrass.

If you are interested in participating in this exciting project to define and protect scenic byways in the Bluegrass, please contact me at The Kentucky Heritage Council in Frankfort, Kentucky (502/564-7005) no later than Monday, September 28th. Thank you for your consideration of this invitation. I look forward to hearing from you soon.

Sincerely,

Susan Yessin

Appendix B

Photographic and Videographic Standards

The issue of environmental sampling is of great importance to the study of perception and preference. Sampling the environment photographically is often more efficient and desirable than placing people directly in the actual landscape. For each visual experience classification, the study must include several representative samples of consistent climatic and light conditions.

Photographic and Videographic Parameters

These suggestions produced the best results in the two case study areas:

- *Color versus Black-and-White.* Color is preferred because it provides the viewer with more information (Nassauer, 1983).
- *Angle of Shooting.* Eye-level views from an automobile are preferred to a tripod parallel to the ground plane (Nassauer, 1983). The latter may not accurately represent the viewing experience. For video, the recommended camera angle of shooting from the automobile is 45 to 60 degrees (0 degrees is parallel to the road of travel and 90 degrees is perpendicular to the road of travel) (Seidler, 1992).
- *Speed of Shooting for Videotaping.* For filming purposes, the driver of the videographer should maintain speeds of approximately 20 miles per hour on dirt roads and 30 miles per hour on paved roads. Slower speeds are necessary to adequately capture not only the conditions of the immediate roadway but the adjacent landscape as well.
- *Lens.* To best represent the horizontal angle, a wide angle (35 mm) is preferred by the experts in the field (Nassauer, 1983). The widest focal length should be used (smaller mm number). For example, on a 10 to 100 mm lens the big picture is seen at 10 mm and the far away object is pulled into view at 100 mm and magnified. A wider focal length will also reduce the turbulence and provide a more stable video (Seidler, 1992).

- *Medium.* Researchers prefer color slides over prints because they more accurately represent the experience in the field due to the function of scale. Video was the medium of preference in the Red Hills case study due to the transitory experience of the visual classifications; vista points or places for static viewing of the landscape were not studied. The landscape of study was viewed at moving speeds (20–55 m.p.h.). The desired format is high resolution, easy operation, durable, small, serviceable, and cost efficient (Seidler, 1992).

- *Film.* Consistently use the same type of film. The best type of film is one that can accommodate a broad range of light conditions.

- *Lighting.* To ensure similar lighting, shoot under the same climatic and light conditions, preferably slightly overcast to cloud-free days. Shoot with the sun on your back, illuminating the foreground, between the hours of 10:30 a.m. and 3:30 p.m. *Caution*: Top light (overhead light), such as bright spots (sun) in the picture area, will deplete the color and detail in the shooting area.

- *Selection and Composition.* Try to control the variables that influence the representation of the visual experience classifications (Kaplan and Kaplan, 1989):

  (1) Avoid photographic imperfections;
  (2) Avoid scenes with striking content which most other scenes do not have;
  (3) Avoid selecting only aesthetically pleasing scenes when sampling a landscape type;
  (4) Use several scenes (four to five) to represent each landscape type;
  (5) Know the territory, that is, the locations of the landscape types;
  (6) Decide whether or not to use close-ups or details;
  (7) Decide about variables of seasonal and climatic conditions.

Appendix C

Sample Visual Unit Classification Questionnaires

Take A Minute!

Scenic Advisory Panel

PLEASE CATEGORIZE EACH PHOTOGRAPH BY CIRCLING A,B,C, D, E, F, G, H, G, H, OR I THROUGHOUT THE FOLLOWING QUESTIONS.

A. Traditional Thoroughbred Horse Farming
B. Modern Thoroughbred Horse Farming
C. Diversified Agriculture
D. Mixed Uses or Transition Zones
E. Piano Key Communities
F. Clusters or Villages
G. Enclosed Road Corridor
H. Open Road Corridor
I. Woodland Pasture/Savanna

1.	A.	B.	C.	D.	E.	F.	G.	H.	I.
2.	A.	B.	C.	D.	E.	F.	G.	H.	I.
3.	A.	B.	C.	D.	E.	F.	G.	H.	I.
4.	A.	B.	C.	D.	E.	F.	G.	H.	I.
5.	A.	B.	C.	D.	E.	F.	G.	H.	I.
6.	A.	B.	C.	D.	E.	F.	G.	H.	I.
7.	A.	B.	C.	D.	E.	F.	G.	H.	I.
8.	A.	B.	C.	D.	E.	F.	G.	H.	I.
9.	A.	B.	C.	D.	E.	F.	G.	H.	I.
10.	A.	B.	C.	D.	E.	F.	G.	H.	I.
11.	A.	B.	C.	D.	E.	F.	G.	H.	I.
12.	A.	B.	C.	D.	E.	F.	G.	H.	I.
13.	A.	B.	C.	D.	E.	F.	G.	H.	I.
14.	A.	B.	C.	D.	E.	F.	G.	H.	I.
15.	A.	B.	C.	D.	E.	F.	G.	H.	I.
16.	A.	B.	C.	D.	E.	F.	G.	H.	I.
17.	A.	B.	C.	D.	E.	F.	G.	H.	I.
18.	A.	B.	C.	D.	E.	F.	G.	H.	I.
19.	A.	B.	C.	D.	E.	F.	G.	H.	I.
20.	A.	B.	C.	D.	E.	F.	G.	H.	I.

APPENDIX 3B

SAMPLE VISUAL UNIT CLASSIFICATION QUESTIONNAIRE

SCENIC ADVISORY PANEL

PLEASE CATEGORIZE EACH VIDEO IMAGE BY THE FOLLOWING CATEGORIES:

OPEN - areas that are expansive in their visual scale by topography, vegetation, and embankments so that the views are long down the road corridor and open, filtered to screened into the landscape. No canopy cover, or adjacent cutbanks occur along these "improved" paved two and four lane roads with wide grassy verges.

PATCHY - areas that are broken up in their visual scale by topography, vegetation, and embankments, so that the views are medium length down the road corridor and predominantly filtered, with open gaps and screened segments of adjacent views. The degree of enclosure or openness varies with sporadic canopy, remnant cutbanks and narrow grassy verges along these paved two lane roads.

ENCLOSED - areas that are confined or constricted in their visual scale by topography, vegetation, and embankments so that the views are short down the road corridor and screened to filtered focusing primarily on the foreground. The degree of enclosure may vary from dense overhead canopy, and steep cutbanks and drainage ditches defining a red clay dirt road; to partial canopy, no cutbanks but still very narrow shoulders bordering paved two lane roads.

Image 1.	Open ( )	Patchy ( )	Enclosed ( )
Image 2.	Open ( )	Patchy ( )	Enclosed ( )
Image 3.	Open ( )	Patchy ( )	Enclosed ( )
Image 4.	Open ( )	Patchy ( )	Enclosed ( )
Image 5.	Open ( )	Patchy ( )	Enclosed ( )
Image 6.	Open ( )	Patchy ( )	Enclosed ( )

Appendix D

Sample Visual Preference and Demographic Questionnaire

Residents of the Bluegrass Take A Minute!

The Bluegrass will face many changes within the next few years. The population will grow as more and more people want to make their home here. The residents of the Bluegrass have expressed an interest in retaining the quality of life that makes this place special. One way to help insure that protection is to identify public resources and design for their protection and enhancement.

We at the Kentucky Heritage Council and Trust for Public Land are looking at the scenic resources unique to this region. Please help us identify and evaluate these resources, as seen from public roads. The results of this questionnaire will be made public for your information.

PLEASE CIRCLE 1 - 5 FOR EACH PHOTOGRAPH DEPENDING ON HOW WELL YOU LIKE IT; 5 MEANS YOU LIKE IT A GREAT DEAL AND 1 MEANS YOU DO NOT LIKE IT AT ALL.
NOTE THAT THE NUMBERING IS NOT CONSECUTIVE. TAKE CARE TO MATCH THE PHOTOGRAPH NUMBER WITH THE QUESTION NUMBER.

		a great deal				not at all
Photo 4.	How much do you like this scene for whatever reason?	5	4	3	2	1
Photo 9.	How much do you like this scene for whatever reason?	5	4	3	2	1
Photo 10.	How much do you like this scene for whatever reason?	5	4	3	2	1
Photo 12.	How much do you like this scene for whatever reason?	5	4	3	2	1
Photo 13.	How much do you like this scene for whatever reason?	5	4	3	2	1
Photo 14.	How much do you like this scene for whatever reason?	5	4	3	2	1
Photo 15.	How much do you like this scene for whatever reason?	5	4	3	2	1
Photo 16.	How much do you like this scene for whatever reason?	5	4	3	2	1
Photo 17.	How much do you like this scene for whatever reason?	5	4	3	2	1
Photo 19.	How much do you like this scene for whatever reason?	5	4	3	2	1
Photo 20.	How much do you like this scene for whatever reason?	5	4	3	2	1
Photo 21.	How much do you like this scene for whatever reason?	5	4	3	2	1
Photo 22.	How much do you like this scene for whatever reason?	5	4	3	2	1
Photo 23.	How much do you like this scene for whatever reason?	5	4	3	2	1

Please fill out the following questions by circling the appropriate response.

1. How old are you?

   less than 20   20 - 40   40 - 60   over 60

2. What gender are you?

   M   F

3. What is your ethnic background?

   American Indian   Asian   Black   White   Hispanic

4. What is your approximate household income?

   0 - 20 thousand   21 - 40 thousand   41 - 70 thousand   over 71 thousand

5. What are your years of schooling?

   Up to High School   Some College   Some Graduate level College

6. What are your favorite activities?

   ____

   ____

7. What is your favorite road or area to drive?

   ____

   ____

9. Mark an X on the Map below approximately where you live.

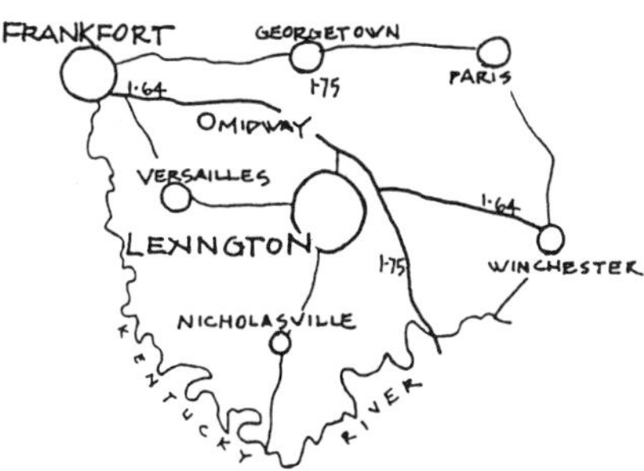

Thank You for your participation!

Appendix E

Sources of Funding, Technical Information, and Assistance

Sources Listed in Chapters 3 and 4

Agricultural Stabilization and Conservation Service, local offices are listed in the phone book under United States Government, Department of Agriculture.

Soil Conservation Service, local offices are listed in the phone book under United States Government, Department of Agriculture.

United States Geological Survey, Eastern Mapping Center, 536 National Center, 12201 Sunrise Valley Drive, Reston, Virginia 22092.

Sources Listed in Chapter 6

The National Park Service (Washington Office and regional offices) provide technical assistance for historic landscape preservation including National Heritage Corridors. United States Department of the Interior, National Park Service, P.O. Box 37127, Washington, D.C. 20013-7127.

The National Headquarters and seven regional offices of the National Trust for Historic Preservation. The National Trust for Historic Preservation, 1785 Massachusetts Avenue, N.W., Washington, D.C. 20036 (202) 673-4037. See The National Trust for Historic Preservation Information Bulletin No. 68 (1992), *The Protection of America's Scenic Byways*, by Shelley Mastran, for additional information on the designation, protection, promotion, and funding of historic and scenic byways and organizations and agencies that deal with these issues.

Scenic America, 21 Dupont Circle, N.W., Washington, D.C. 20036.

The Land Trust Alliance, 1319 F Street N.W., Suite 501, Washington, D.C. 20004.

The Trust for Public Land, 116 New Montgomerey Street, Fourth Floor, San Francisco, California 94105.

Apalachee Land Conservancy, 2424 West Lake Shore Drive, Tallahassee, Florida 32312 (904) 385-7997.

Lexington-Frankfort Scenic Corridor, Inc., 4600 Old Frankfort Pike, Lexington, Kentucky 40510.

Low Country Open Land Trust, P.O. Box 1293, Charleston, South Carolina 29402.

Chattahoochee-Flint Regional Development Center, 13273 Georgia Highway 34 East, P.O. Box 1600, Franklin, Georgia 30217.

Tallahassee-Leon County Planning Department, City Hall, 300 South Adams Street, Tallahassee, Florida 32301 (904) 891-8600.

Bibliography

Canopy Roads Citizens Committee. 1992. *Canopy Roads Management Plan.* Tallahassee-Leon County (Florida) Planning Commission.

Carlson, Christine and Steven Durrant. 1985. *The Farm Landscape of Whatcomb County.* Department of Landscape Architecture, JO-34, University of Washington, Seattle, Washington 98195.

Ceo, Rocco J. and Margot Ammidown. 1993. *Redland: A Preservation and Tourism Plan.* University of Miami School of Architecture and the Metro Dade Historic Preservation Division. Miami, Florida.

Copps, David H. 1993. *A Scenic Assessment of Old Frankfort and Pisgah Pikes (Draft).* The Trust for Public Land, Southeast Regional Office, Tallahassee, Florida.

Copps, David H., Joy Dorst, and Kevin McGorty. 1993. *The Red Hills Historic and Scenic Road Assessment (Draft).* The Trust for Public Land, Southeast Regional Office, Tallahassee, Florida.

Davis, George D. and Thomas R. Duffus. 1987. *Developing a Land Conservation Strategy, A Handbook for Land Trusts.* Adirondack Land Trust, Elizabethtown, New York.

Derry, Anne, H., Ward Jandl, Carol D. Shull, Jan Thorman, and Patricia Parker. 1985. *Guidelines for Local Surveys: A Basis for Preservation Planning.* United States Department of the Interior, National Park Service, National Register of Historic Places, Washington, D.C.

East, W. Gordon. 1965. *The Geography Behind History.* W.W. Norton and Company, Inc., New York.

Fairbrother, Nan. 1970. *New Lives, New Landscapes.* Alfred Knopf, New York.

Frost, Jane R. and Kate Stenberg. 1992. *Designing Wetlands Preservation Programs for Local Governments: A Guide to Non-Regulatory Protection.* Washington State Department of Ecology in Cooperation with King County. Publication #92-18.

Gilbert, Cathy. 1985. *Reading the Cultural Landscape: Ebey's Landing National Historical Reserve.* National Park Service, Pacific Northwest Regional Office, Cultural Resource Division, Seattle, Washington.

Harper, D.B. 1978. *Guidelines for Identifying and Evaluating a Scenic Resource.* New York State Department of Environmental Conservation.

Hiss, Tony. 1990. *The Experience of Place.* Alfred Knopf, New York.

Jahoda, Gloria. 1967. *The Other Florida.* Scribner's Sons, New York.

Kaplan, R. and S. Kaplan. 1989. *The Experience of Nature: A Psychological Perspective.* Cambridge Press, Cambridge, Massachusetts.

Knutson, Roger M. 1987. *Flattened Fauna.* Ten Speed Press, Berkeley, California.

Lubar, Steven. 1991. "West Old Baltimore Road." *Landscape* 31(1).

Mantell, Micheal A., Stephen F. Harper, and Luther Propst. The Conservation Foundation. 1990. *Creating Successful Communities: A Guidebook to Growth Management Strategies.* Island Press, Washington, D.C.

_________. 1990. *Resource Guide for Creating Successful Communities.* Island Press, Washington, D.C.

Mastran, Shelley. 1992. *The Protection of America's Scenic Byways*. The National Trust for Historic Preservation. Information Series No. 68.

McClelland, Linda F. 1991. "Imagery, Ideals, and Social Values: The Interpretation and Documentation of Cultural Landscapes." *The Public Historian* 13(2).

McClelland, Linda F., J. Timothy Keller, Genevieve P. Keller, and Robert Z. Melnick. 1990. *Guidelines for Evaluating and Documenting Rural Historic Landscapes: National Register Bulletin 30.* United States Department of the Interior, National Park Service, National Register of Historic Places, Washington, D.C.

Melnick, Robert Z. 1984. *Cultural Landscapes: Rural Historic Districts in the National Park System.* U.S. Department of Interior, National Park Service, Washington, D.C.

Nassauer, J. I. 1983. "Framing the Landscape in Photographic Simulation." *Journal of Environmental Management* 17: 1-16.

National Trust for Historic Preservation. 1994. *Community Guide to Corridor Management Planning* (draft). Federal Highway Administration, Washington, D.C.

Noe, Francis P. and William E. Hammitt (eds.). 1988. *Visual Preferences of Travelers Along the Blue Ridge Parkway*. National Park Service, U.S. Department of Interior, Government Printing Office, Washington, D.C.

The Report of the President's Commission. 1987. *Americans Outdoors*. Island Press, Washington, D.C.

Risch, Laurie, Susan Cabot, Billie Cahill, and Greg Harper. 1992. *Northern Kentucky Historic Back Roads Tour*. Picture This! Books, 75 Sunnymede Dr., Ft. Mitchell, Kentucky 41017.

Rogers, James, Ben Chandler, and Toss Chandler. 1989. *As We Were, As We Are: A Tour Guide of Woodford County Kentucky*. The Woodford County Woman's Club, Versailles, Kentucky.

Scenic America. 1993. *Fact Sheet: Designation of State Scenic Byways*. Washington, D.C.

__________. 1994. *Preparing Corridor Management Plans: A Scenic Byways Guidebook* (draft). Federal Highway Administration, Washington, D.C.

Schauman, Sally. 1988. "Scenic Value of Countryside Landscapes to Local Residents: A Whatcomb County, Washington Case Study." *Landscape Journal* 7(1): 40-46.

Seidler, Robert. 1992. *Videographic Standards for "Views from the Road Project."* Seidler Productions, Inc., St. Marks, Florida.

Shanahan, Deborah and Richard Smardon. 1988. *Preserving New York State Scenic Roads, A Guide to Designation*. New York State Department of Environmental Conservation.

Stilgoe, John R. 1982. *Common Landscape of America, 1580 to 1845*. Yale University, New Haven, Connecticut.

Stokes, Samuel N., A. Elizabeth Watson, Genevieve P. Keller, and J. Timothy Keller for the National Trust for Historic Preservation. 1989. *Saving America's Countryside: A Guide to Rural Conservation*. The John Hopkins University Press, Baltimore, Maryland.

Tait, J., A. Lane, and S. Carr. 1988. *Practical Conservation: Site Assessment and Management*. The Open University in Association with the Nature Conservancy Council. Milton Keynes, Great Britain.

U.S. Department of Agriculture. Forest Service. 1983. *National Forest Landscape Management, Timber*. Agricultural Handbook 559. U.S. Government Printing Office, Washington, D.C.

U.S. Department of Agriculture. Soil Conservation Service. 1985. *Field Guide for Assessing Scenic Quality in Countryside Landscapes (Draft)*. West National Technical Center, Portland, Oregon.

U.S. Department of Transportation. Federal Highway Administration. 1991. *National Scenic Byway Study*. Publication No. PD-91-010.

Whyte, William H. 1968. *The Last Landscape*. Doubleday, New York.

Notes

1 Beach, Virginia. 1992. "Buffer Easements: Preserving Scenic Byways." *Views and Vistas. Newsletter of the Low Country Open Land Trust* 3(2): 1

2 McClelland, Linda F., J. Timothy Keller, Genevieve P. Keller, and Robert Z. Melnick. 1990. *Guidelines for Evaluating and Documenting Rural Historic Landscapes: National Register Bulletin 30.* United States Department of the Interior, National Park Service, National Register of Historic Places, Washington, D.C., p. 3.

3 Stilgoe, John R. 1982. *Common Landscape of America, 1580 to 1845.* Yale University, New Haven, Connecticut.

4 Lubar, Steven. 1991. "West Old Baltimore Road." *Landscape* 31(1): 20.

5 Jahoda, Gloria. 1967. *The Other Florida.* Scribner's Sons, New York, p. 160.

6 Gilbert, Cathy. 1985. *Reading the Cultural Landscape: Ebey's Landing National Historical Reserve.* National Park Service, Pacific Northwest Regional Office, Cultural Resource Division, Seattle, Washington, p. 27

7 McClelland *et al.*, op. cit. note 2.

8 East, W. Gordon. 1965. *The Geography Behind History.* W.W. Norton and Company, Inc, New York, p. 3.

9 Kaplan, R. and S. Kaplan. 1989. *The Experience of Nature: A Psychological Perspective.* Cambridge Press, Cambridge, Massachusetts.

10 Ibid.

11 Land Trust Alliance. 1991. *National Directory of Conservation Land Trusts*, p. iv.

Index

About the Author

David H. Copps is a field representative for the Conservation Services Program at the Trust for Public Land, Southeast Region. He received his master's degree in landscape architecture from the University of Georgia and is a member of the American Society of Landscape Architects.